MAN

THE PERENNIAL QUESTION

(Studies in Theological Anthropology)

Morris A. Inch

Robert Webber

University Press of America, ® **Inc.**
Lanham • New York • Oxford

Copyright © 1999
University Press of America,® Inc.
4720 Boston Way
Lanham, Maryland 20706

12 Hid's Copse Rd.
Cumnor Hill, Oxford OX2 9JJ

Library of Congress Cataloging-in-Publication Data

Inch, Morris A.
Man : the perennial question : studies in theological anthropology /
Morris A. Inch.
p.   cm.
Includes bibliographical references.
1. Theology. 2. Man (Christian theology) I. Title.
BR85.I55   1998   233—dc21   98-48618 CIP

ISBN 0-7618-1303-9 (pbk: alk. ppr.)

Contents

Acknowledgment

I should like to express a special word of appreciation to my cherished wife Joan not only for editing and formatting the text, but her continued encouragement.

Preface

I have been asked from time to time if there is some topic that served as a common denominator for my writing. Qualifications aside, it would be a theological understanding of man (meant in its generic sense of embracing male and female). This was anticipated by my first book: *Psychology in the Psalms* (1969).

The following articles are arranged by time periods. First, we return to the sometimes turbulent *Sixties*, initiated at the beginning of that decade and extending to the middle of the next. After this, we proceed with a time frame closing with 1986, when I took up overseas assignments--first in Israel and then in Romania. Finally, we follow our course to the present.

This collection of articles helps to fill in the gaps among the various books I have published over the years. While several appeared separately in one periodical or another, they come together for the first time in the present volume--along with other entries. As for the latter, whereas some were read at professional gatherings, we encounter others for the first time.

"What is man?" inquires the psalmist (8:4). Thomas Huxley characterizes this as *the question of questions*. As such, appears so pervasive as implicated in all other inquiries, so intensive as to demand our attempt to answer, and so extensive as to persist regardless of changing times and circumstances. It is especially in the last connection that we discover its *perennial* character.

THE *SIXTIES*

As mentioned earlier, the *Sixties* may be said to extend from the start of that decade through the middle of the subsequent one. It was a period of social upheaval, which underscored the need to get our individual and corporate identity into focus.

Since we were experiencing difficulty reaching a functional consensus, I focused on the classic Jesus paradigm (cf. Heb. 2:9). As with Wolfhart Pannenberg, I assumed that this would require that we commence with the Jesus of history, proceed with His transcendence, and finish off with His immanent character.

The Apologetic Use of Sign in the Fourth Gospel confronts us with the Jesus of history. *Jesus as Lord!* enlarges on some implications of His transcendence. The remaining two articles extend the task of constructing the Jesus paradigm: *Matthew and the House-Churches* with regard to the faith community, and *The Transcendence of God and An Open Future* concerning the hope dynamic of living toward the future. The first and third articles formerly appeared in *The Evangelical Quarterly*, the second in the *Journal of the Evangelical Theological Society*, and the fourth in the *Christian Scholar's Review*.

THE APOLOGETIC USE OF *SIGN* IN THE FOURTH GOSPEL*

Martin Marty, distinguished University of Chicago professor, heralds a new day for Christian apologetics. If true, this may be an announcement that Christianity has survived the crisis in secular theology as well as escaped the archaic and inflexible mold of Christendom. It is within the framework of such a possibility, where signs may again be evidence rather than embarrassment, that we entertain the following considerations.

Sign and Meaning

Sign is the means by which Christ's claim is commended for believing response (John 20:30-31). John seems bent on underscoring the rationale and reality of Christian experience. Apologetics is consequently for him no less than *a considered faith.*

John moreover expresses a concern to commend his faith to others. Those who read his words were already far removed from the scene of Jesus' public ministry, insensitive to the impact of His personal dynamic, and incredulous of reports which had been circulated. John wishes to bridge the chasm with appropriate evidence for faith to negotiate. Thus we may conclude that apologetics is not only a considered but considerate expression of faith (cf. 1 Pet. 3:15).

The signs are selected (20:30) and abridged (21:25). It is the Person and efficacious words of Christ, rather than His performance and wonder, which proves central to John's message (20:31). So the signs were not meant to confound but reveal, not as entries in Ripley's *Believe It or Not,* but the gospel's *that you might believe.*

Signs do not convey self-evident meaning. The resurrection of a man from the dead would be subject to endless speculation. What made Jesus' revival so unique was that it came against the background of a messianic

*Reprinted by permission of *The Evangelical Quarterly.*

preparation and as fulfillment. That is, it was not an extraordinary event in what was otherwise an ordinary life within an equally undistinguished religious tradition. The resurrection was the climax to a profound interpretation of history, based upon a divine revelation-human response theme.

The point is aptly illustrated in Jesus' discussion with the Samaritan woman (4:1-42). He engages her interest through the promise of life enrichment, nourishes it by way of revealing a confidence, and climaxes the interaction with His claim to be the Messiah. As a result, the woman gathered a company which after sitting under Jesus' teaching for two days, confessed to the woman: "It is no longer because of what you said that we believe, for we have heard for ourselves and know that this One is indeed the Savior of the world" (4:42).

The account of the excommunicated enthusiast is to similar intent (9:1-10, 21). Jesus rejects the alternatives that the man's blindness results from either personal or parental evil, and describes it as the occasion for God's restorative work. The man's physical condition responds immediately, and his spiritual sight gradually--from a faint glimmering into *one called Jesus* (9:11) to the dazzling recognition *Lord I believe* (9:38).

His confession provided an exit from the synagogue (9:22), but entrance into abundant life (10:10). Jesus proceeds by way of the humanistic qualities of the Christian faith, the healing aspects of life lived in response to divine challenge. In response to antagonism, He asks that His claim be compared to the teaching of Scripture (10:34-36) and the testimony of His good works (10:37-38). If you will, there was a convergence of evidence with a locus of meaning.

To this might be added the witness of those schooled by John the Baptist: "While John performed no sign, yet everything John said about this man was true" (10:41). Many believed as a result. That is, life fitted into a messianic setting, both in its extent--as a redemptive interpretation of history, and its extension--the particular incidents of Jesus' ministry as correlation of the prophetic testimony. Christ brought into focus *all* of life, and into relationship *each* aspect of it. The sign did not stand as a bizarre interjection, but a meaningful unity of divine revelation and human appropriation.

Sign Without Faith

Neither faith nor sign stand alone. Faith is the context of sign, and sign is the text of faith. John pictures the crass multitude as demanding signs to self-activate faith (6:30-31). Jesus refrained. Instead, He emphasized the importance of cultivating a vital relationship with the Master. Similarly, when beseeched by a royal official on behalf of his critically ill son, Jesus chided him for requiring signs and wonders (4:48). Perhaps driven to a deeper level of apprehension and/or concern, the ruler plead for the life of his son. No sign was forthcoming except Jesus' *word* that the son would live. The man departed in belief, and to find that his faith was honored.

Faith consequently does not have to look for signs, but to the Savior. There is something undesirable about demanding wonders for the purpose of initiating or bolstering faith. A personal instance comes to mind in this connection. It happened one morning as I was shaving, and mused over my ineffectiveness in a struggling church. Then, as clearly as if someone were standing in the room, I heard: "Do not be weary in well doing, for in due season you shall reap, if you do not faint."

It was a startling experience. I looked around, but there was no one there. I went to the door, to determine if my wife might be playing a trick on me. She was not to be seen. Remembering Augustine hearing the voice of a child, I peered out the window--even though it opened from the second story.

Had there been someone with me, would they have heard the voice? I doubt it. I am not even convinced that God would use the King James Version to quote Scripture. Regardless of how it might be explained, I suspect that God meant to encourage me. Whatever else might be implied, it was not evidence of my great spirituality but disabling despair. I concluded that God had spoken when I was not attentive to His gentle prompting.

Otherwise stated, John's apologetic stresses *witness* not to the exclusion of *wonder*, but as his focus. Signs are merely means in God's providence and not ends to be cultivated either to assure faith or indicate spirituality. All things considered, we do better to foster the most excellent way of love (1 Cor. 12:31) rather than manufacture the mysterious.

Dietrich Bonhoeffer's *world come of age* may be pertinent in this connection, for Twentieth Century man seems more concerned for responsible maturity than with a religious sleight of hand. He is more impressed with faith giving evidence than in evidence compelling faith.

Faith Without Sign

Even so, *faith* unlike *credulity* does not disregard evidence; *faith* unlike *credulity* must do its home work. John therefore takes us back to the first of Jesus' signs, the miraculous provision for the marriage festival at Cana of Galilee (2:1-11). In this connection, Jesus' disciples were encouraged to put their faith in the Master (2:11). Others seem not involved, except for the servants who were aware of what transpired.

The clandestine nature of the event is explained by the comment: "My hour has not yet come" (2:4). The subsequent signs would be more or less public in nature, dependent upon the phase of Jesus' ministry--more characteristic of the Synoptic Gospels, and the unique preparation of individuals--more illustrative of John's alternative.

The private nature of the sign is additionally in sharp contrast to the public use John makes of it. The situation has changed, altering the purpose to which the evidence may be employed. As such, the sign serves in one connection or another, depending on the need of the moment.

John does not mean to foster doubt concerning Jesus' use of signs. The multitude was attracted to Him for that reason (6:2), and those who believed inquired: "When the Christ shall come, He will not perform more signs than those which this man does, will He?" (7:31). Even the chief priests and Pharisees acknowledged that since so many signs were done that all might be swept away in a surge of faith, an event of such magnitude as to endanger their standing with the Roman authorities (11:48). Thus it would seem that their decision to have Jesus killed was indirectly tied to their inability to discredit His signs.

Later on, Talmudic writers attributed the signs to magic. For instance, "And it is tradition: on the eve of Pesah they hung Jeshu. And the crier went forth before him forty days, (saying Yeshuah) goes forth to be stoned, because he has practiced magic and deceived and lead astray Israel" (*Sanhedrin* 48a). The signs will not in any case go away, remaining to be negotiated either by faith or doubt.

Sign and the Psychology of Disbelief

The most extensive of John's signs were the raising of Lazarus and the resurrection of Jesus. This fits well with his emphasis on eternal and abundant life, and invites our more careful scrutiny.

Marcus Dods, alone among those commentators consulted, picks up the apologetic thrust of Jesus' resurrection with the account of Lazarus. He concludes that Jesus is revealed as the Christ through His friend's revival: its impact felt first among those associated with Lazarus (12:1-11), then with the people generally (12:12-19), and finally with the Gentiles inquiring of Jesus (12:20-36).

The sign, thus understood, serves to demonstrate the persuasive character of Jesus' messianic claim:

1. It was known to Lazarus' associates. The report was not a matter of hearsay or some garbled tradition. Those best acquainted with the facts attested to the sign and its significance. Many traveled not only to hear Jesus, but to see the man who had been raised from the dead (12:9).

2. It triggered the populace's support of Jesus. John presses the issue deftly: "So the multitude who were with him when he called Lazarus out of the tomb and raised him from the dead, were bearing him witness," and adds, "for this cause also the multitude went and met him, because they heard that he had performed this sign" (12:17-18). The fact could not be ignored, and the clamor has not altogether subsided with the passing of time.

3. It initiated Gentile interest. John was not unmindful of the differences in religious background between Jews and their pagan neighbors. Time had already illustrated Jesus' appeal across religious/cultural boundaries, and John affirms that it was so from the beginning. It suggests that the implications of the Lazarus sign were meant not simply for a particular religious tradition but all people everywhere.

Then, why did not all believe? As a matter of fact, "though he had performed so many signs before them, they were not believing in him" (12:37). John's answer would in brief appear to be that evidence commends but does not coerce faith.

Is his rationale plausible for today? Qualifications notwithstanding, I suspect so. In any case, John's elaboration follows two lines: the blindness that plagues our human condition (12:40), and the pressure of society (12:42-43).

As for the former, John refers us to Isaiah 6. Herein, we read of the prophet's vision of a holy God, arousing his sense of guilt, leading to subsequent cleansing, and his readiness to serve as God's messenger--only to be warned of the resistance he can expect. Likewise implied, should the light-giving word be rejected, we may expect an even more oppressive darkness to settle in.

An analogy has proven helpful to me. A person comes in off a darkened street into a brightly lighted room. His/her first reaction is to turn away. It would be more comfortable in the darkness to which one was accustomed. However, if he/she allows time to adjust, the wait will be rewarded. The test requires that we tolerate momentary discomfort for the gain anticipated.

Human nature is like that. It relishes darkness, and turns from the light. As often the case, the person enters a counselor's office, talks about everything but the issue, and finally gets down to the crux of the matter. The moment of decision is fast approaching, and with it, the temptation to flee. If one turns back now, it will be to a situation more desperate than before. If he/she musters the courage to proceed, all will be well. Now the counselor is called upon to make every reasonable effort to see the person through this critical juncture.

Some issues are relatively insignificant, so that the *status quo syndrome* is of little consequence. Not so when a divine imperative is involved, such as implied with Thomas' confession "My Lord and my God" (20:28), and its corollary "that believing you may have life in His name" (20:31). Herewith, the light from which man may recoil (12:40) or respond (20:31) is the incarnated luminary of God (12:45). John explains: "For everyone who does evil hates the light, and does not come to the light lest his deed should be exposed. But he who practices the truth comes to the light, that his deed may be manifested as having been wrought in God" (3:20-21). Given the traumatic proportions of such an encounter, Jesus assures us that His purpose in coming was not to condemn but redeem mankind (3:17).

Can we account for disbelief simply on the above grounds? Not according to John. There remains the inhibitions fostered by society (12:42-43). Some believed but were reluctant to express their belief for fear of how others would respond. This, in turn, impacted negatively on those who might have otherwise come to faith.

The social factor was perhaps involved with Nicodemus coming to Jesus *by night*, though he freely acknowledged the signs as being of divine origin (3:2). He might well have feared the response of the religious authorities otherwise, and there is no more severe a social sanction than that said to be exercised at God's bequest. Persons thereby are threatened not only with retribution in this life, but damnation for eternity.

It turns out that such darkness as described persists both intensively within human nature, and extensively in corporate situations. Jesus describes such as *the world*: the human system fostered to perpetuate man's opposition to God, and frustrate His righteous purposes (cf. 15:19). It breeds hate for all that is unlike itself (15:25), and demands that Jesus be crucified (19:15).

Sign and Salvation

The second sign John treats at considerable length is the resurrection of Jesus. It was God's emphatic *yes* to man's persistent *no*. It was the vindication of the Almighty over the vindictiveness of the world. It was of cosmic proportions, so that Paul insists that men everywhere must in connection with the resurrection repent (Acts 17:30).

The transition from futility to faith in John's narrative is grand. Mary Magdalene weeps in the garden for she does not know where Jesus' body has been taken. A figure stands by her, asking the cause for her sorrow and the purpose for her presence. She recognizes Him with reverential compassion: *Rabboni.* Jesus cautions her against restraining Him, for He has a task to complete. After this, Mary rushes off to the disciples with the glad announcement: "I have seen the Lord!" (20:11-18).

Thomas' case is even more striking. He had been absent at Jesus' first appearing to the disciples, and protested: "Unless I shall see in His hands the imprint of the nails, and put my finger into the place of the nails, and put my hand into His side, I will not believe." The disciples again were gathered in the closed room when Jesus appears. He is aware of Thomas' altercation, and offers His body as confirmation of the sign. There follows the sublime confession: "My Lord and my God," to which Jesus pointedly replies: "Because you have seen Me, have you believed? Blessed are they who have not seen but believe" (20:19-29).

John draws at least one and probably two conclusions from the resurrection. The first is manifest. It is that man may believe (20:29-31). Faith is appropriate not on the basis of one remarkable event, but as it serves as the capstone to the divine affusion of light (1:1-18). The latter was a moral miracle of life and testimony, the purity of which the world has never otherwise experienced nor could reproduce.

Reflecting back, the disciples had difficulty understanding Jesus' warning of His impending death. This did not fit in with their idea of a royal Messiah, and for most, the thought was crowded from their minds. Thomas was perhaps unique in allowing Jesus' words to sink in; whereupon, he urged: "Let us also go, that we may die with him" (11:16). His was a *practical* faith that could accept anything up to and including death. Conversely, it could not manage further.

That is, not without help from the resurrection. The latter demonstrated that death was vanquished, and eternal life a credible opportunity. It did not demand faith, but made it accessible to those who would weigh the matter seriously.

Less obvious, John seems to suggest that we can act in loving constraint with resurrection faith (21:1-23). He describes in this connection the restless return of the disciples to fishing, their lack of success, the appearing of Jesus, success following His instruction, breakfast by the seaside, and the three-way discussion among Jesus, Peter, and John. The play on *phileo* and *agapao* in the interchange probably suggests a missing but potential dimension to Peter's love, a theme which would characterize the Johannine Epistles.

Agape provides the necessary ingredient to following Jesus. It is the creative aspect of devotion, flowing as if from an internal spring and independent of the response of others. Peter would soon experience situations beyond his control, and would have to rely on spiritual resources made available to him.

The very call of Jesus implies a possibility of realization, as if an opportunity for faith to embrace its potential. John subsequently leaves the discussion at the point of personal stewardship, without recourse to the failure of another as our excuse (21:23). There is moreover a timelessness to the appeal, which confronts people in whatever situation they find themselves.

This spins off into a freedom born of love. If free in this world, we are in fact in bondage (8:34); if free in Christ, we are genuinely free (8:36). We are free to love God, and free to love one another. We are also free to love those who return evil for good.

An apologetic that stops short of moral transformation would seem poor consolation indeed. It would dangle before perishing humanity an ideal incapable of being realized. John would assure us otherwise. He would have us know not only the way of salvation but experience its power.

Postscript

Twentieth Century man may not actually have come of age, as Dietrich Bonhoeffer supposed, but he has come far. His capabilities are from a technological perspective quite astonishing. He is however not necessarily better as a result. It rather seems as if the stakes have gone up.

As if to satisfy an increased potential, there has come a stress on situation ethics, and a distrust of anything as old as yesterday. Man flounders as a result, lacking the direction and motivation the past could give him. His sense of obligation lacks needed perspective.

There is much to suggest that contemporary man is paying a high price for his self-imposed ignorance. We may be approaching a social psychosis of a magnitude seldom if ever before realized, driven by the realization of a responsibility without rationale.

As a result, we are inclined to surrender the obligations commensurate with our present possibilities. This is especially distressing when found in Christian circles, since we should take our direction from Jesus rather than cultural norms, if in fact, we can discover what they are. If we would follow Jesus, we must remain current and caring, regardless of how others behave (21:21).

Jesus is our vanguard. All else is dated and inhibiting.

The Christian ought to be if not comfortable at least accustomed to change. He/she experiences through Jesus what the innovative Harvard University professor Harvey Cox would describe as *a mobile God.* He leads us from the confines of parochial security to a land of promise. We follow not with fear but faith.

Editorial note. The above assumes that the Jesus of history cannot altogether be divorced from the Christ of faith. Ethelbert Stauffer's *Jesus and His Story* (New York: Knopf, 1960) seemingly takes the distinction just about as far as we can go. I have rather been content to focus on John's gospel narrative, already removed from the events it describes, but prior to the extensive theological tradition that has built subsequent to it. We are thereby primed to turn our attention to the transcendent character of Jesus with the confession that *Jesus is Lord.*

JESUS IS LORD!*

The fundamental confession of Christianity is that *Jesus is Lord.* What that may imply is the subject before us.

* * *

To begin with, we must go back to a scene which has become distorted by time and tradition. "To think again the first Christians' thoughts about Jesus one must be prepared to enter a strange world. Mentally the reader must cross five thousand miles, nineteen centuries, and an even wider gulf of ideas."[1]

We might question whether the hard journey is really necessary. Yes, it most certainly is! The Nineteenth Century lives of Jesus failed at this very point. They turned out to be little more than an author's projection. There resulted as many *jesuses* as there were biographies, while the real Jesus failed to come through. Apart from the discipline to weigh the historical record seriously, we can expect to do no better.

What do we find upon arrival back in the strange surroundings of a yesterday obscured by unfamiliar mores and familiar words rent from context over the intervening years? The first thing is that Jesus taught with authority, in contrast to rabbinic custom. The Hebrew was the first great history people, who used the past to chart a responsible course for the future. Precedent was critical for such a venture. Without it, the past would be lost, and man destined to repeat his follies. With careful concern for former experience, progress could be assured. The rabbis consequently tied commentary to decision and decision to commentary, with a growing body of documented wisdom to guide man's steps.

Then Jesus came teaching: "It has been said of old, but I say to you." The rabbis were offended, and the people astounded. Jesus taught as none other, with an authority assumed by His relationship to the Father. Time has eroded the shock of the Nazarine's *presumption.* Tradition has

*Reprinted by permission of the *Journal of the Evangelical Theological Society.*

made it commonplace. We must go back to feel the impact of a bearing that transcended the need of and expectation for human corroboration. We must consider the unique impact of Jesus' authoritative teaching.

We next observe that Jesus assumed peculiar prerogatives. The Temple, as the unassailable and impregnable focus of social-religious authority,

> must have provided parasitic priests and middlemen with an effective shield against any nonviolent popular protest. It was Jesus' attempt to smash this shield, as part of his larger enterprise of presiding over the Kingdom of God in defiance of the Roman power, that set in motion the events leading to his downfall.[2]

To see in Jesus' aggressiveness simply a violent turn would be to confuse His identification with the populace and distinction from the Zealots. He took the part of the common man while distrusting the sword. The issue lay deeper, as Carmichael surmises, with Jesus' regal position. Others skirted issues out of deference to the religious elite or made a power struggle out of their excesses, but Jesus acted with the objective dispatch of a royal potentate.

Perhaps still more startling to Jesus' contemporaries was the basis on which He claimed authority. It earned Him the charge of blasphemy. Dietrich Bonhoeffer consequently observed: "Jesus' testimony to himself stands by itself, self-authenticating."[3] It does not stand alone, in that the testimony is coupled to preachment and practice, but by itself, as revelation concerning this most distinctive life. Jesus confidently affirmed *I am*, understood as a claim to divine presence. Some hoped to locate an earlier level of Christian teaching behind this testimony, a hero eventually elevated with divine attributes. The effort however has uncovered no such antecedent: "The truth is that it is impossible to penetrate back to a time in the history of the church where the Risen Christ was not looked upon as a Divine Being."[4]

* * *

It remains for us to make explicit what has already been implied concerning the lordship of Jesus. William Ramsay muses: "Perhaps the most interesting of the Messianic titles given to Jesus by the Jerusalem church is the title *Lord*. Those who use it thoughtlessly Sunday after Sunday hardly realize the original significance of this word."[5] The meaning must be derived from that early milieu, unprejudiced by centuries of religious rationalization, where the term was couched in a particular context of regency.

We today may think of royalty as an honorific designation stripped of authority, but not so at that time. It implied for them an authority from which they might benefit. In a comprehensive sense, it symbolized life itself.

With this in mind, we approach the classic commentaries on Jesus' lordship (Col. 1:13-23; Heb. 1). Herein, our attention is drawn to Jesus' ample provision. He provides what we would otherwise lack, and we serve in grateful response to His benevolence and contingent on His grace. That is to say, we cannot out-give God. Only little people fail to see how great things the Lord would do for them.

The same passages imply related responsibilities. Paul's lordship discourse nestles into an account of Christian discipleship, his and that of the Colossian believers. The apostle had received a good report from the church, and commends them further to God--while relating his own determination to press on. The author of Hebrews similarly concludes his commentary with: "For this reason we must pay closer attention to what we have heard, lest we drift away from it" (Heb. 2:1). A prominent Jewish writer struggles with Jesus' uniqueness as follows: "But to *seek out* the sinner, and instead of avoiding the bad companion, to choose him as your friend in order to work his moral redemption, this was, I fancy, something new in the religious history of Israel."[6] "He (Jesus) would quench the evil and quicken the good," Montefiori speculates further, "by giving the sinner somebody to admire and to love. He asked for service, and put it in the place of sin."

"It does not follow that in a lesser man these methods would be either justified or successful," the rabbi concludes. Qualifications aside, he is no doubt correct. Jesus' approach drew from an exalted position as Lord, and cannot be precisely duplicated--however legitimately emulated.

So Jesus was not only here, where men saw and heard Him; but God among us, revealing His transcendent character. He as such assumed a royal prerogative, and held persons responsible for their calling. All things considered, Jesus is Lord!

* * *

While some are reluctant to go back, others hesitate in proceeding in the light of what we have discovered. Whereas the former lose the foundation, the latter frustrate the faith; the one ignores divine presence and the other human potential. As we have resisted the first temptation, we shall attempt to overcome the second as well.

The essence of life is community, and there are irrevocable laws governing it. *Community* implies sharing common conditions, common concerns, and common experience. Man has no life in isolation. He becomes what he is as a result of social interaction. In this manner, life is initiated and subsequently refined. Alienation threatens the fragile fabric which holds life together.

Community does not come about just any old way. It is structured by the mandates (commands) of God. Traditionally we have understood these as relates to family, government, labor, and church.

We shall first want to separate the mandates for purpose of discussion and then consider how they bond together. The family customarily provides the primary socializing agency. With such in view, we ought not to equate intercourse between consenting partners with masturbation, nor reduce family relationships to the exchange of service. It is primarily within the home that we learn the character of unconditional love, and shared obligations.

The Hebrew family extended to include distant relatives and the strangers within the household (Exod. 12:49; Lev. 24:22; Num. 15:15). Even lacking the Hebrew clan associations, something of the ideal was carried over into the Christian accent on hospitality (Rom. 12:13; Titus 1:8; 1 Pet. 4:9). This would seem to suggest that while social structures may vary, we ought not to limit our understanding of family and home to nuclear consideration.

Moving on with a discussion of mandates, political considerations play a prominent role in the Old Testament, and a more vital role than usually imagined in the New Testament. Vladimir Simkhovitch comments in the latter connection:

> The central problem of his people was so enveloping that we can take for granted that Jesus' religious and intellectual life revolved around it.... To repeat, at the given time there was but one problem for the Jews--a single, all-absorbing national problem that became under the circumstances the religious problem as well.[7]

We need not embrace this suggestion without reservation to recognize the important place political concerns played out in Jesus' experience. He lived and labored within a religious establishment, where no sharp distinction could be made between political and religious matters. They were both part of the same *spiritual* concern.

One of the reasons we tend to overlook the political implications of Jesus' life and teaching is because the disciples did not as a rule assume political office, first in the Hebrew context and then in the pagan world. They however responded by pledging support for those in authority

(Rom. 13:12), and waiting such time as conditions would prove more favorable for them to take on a more active role.

As concerns labor, Paul's rule left little to the imagination: "If anyone will not work, neither let him eat" (2 Thess. 3:10). It reflected a deep and abiding respect for constructive enterprise as the means whereby we embrace the responsibility to care for our own needs and those of others. Inasmuch as we bear our own and the burdens of others (Gal. 6:2, 5), none should have to go without while others had more than enough. Conversely, no one should expect that someone do for him what he is unwilling to do for himself.

Work is a duty; work is a privilege; work is a blessing. The economic mandate thus joins that of family and government as a means of cultivating life together.

The mandate concerning church rounds out the short list. It may at first seem strange to include this along with the others, in that it would be thought to pertain to a select group of people. Upon closer observation, this proves not to be the case. Whether we are actively involved or not, we are obligated to God for that which He institutes. As such, we are not to usurp ecclesiastical prerogatives, or otherwise inhibit the church's ministry. We ought rather to accommodate the church's presence among us, and gratefully encourage its activity.

On the other hand, the church is obligated to fulfill its role as a responsible member of society. It should proclaim the gospel, support constructive social endeavor, and be active in meeting the needs of its own fellowship and that of others.

The mandates when taken together structure life as God would have it. Otherwise stated, they flesh out the decalogue. Commenting in another context, I observed that to

> love another as myself is to guarantee him those same prerogatives I desire for myself: the privilege of filial relationship, the opportunity for labor, and justice and mercy from society. That is not enough, however, for it is only as our self-concern is elevated by the love of God that life falls into place.

It occurs to me that we come to much the same conclusion if in place of *love* we approach the topic by way of *reverence/respect*. The latter appears as if foundational for the family (Eph. 5:21), government (Rom. 13:3), labor (2 Thess. 3:11-12), and the church (Eph. 5:24, 33). Now,

> a genuine response to God's love expressed a sincere reverence and

respect for Him in word as well as in the total pattern of daily living. ...Fear in the sense of "being afraid" of God arose only when the vital love relationship expressed in the first two commandments was decimated.[9]

One thing more should be added. The mandates understood individually or collectively are anything but constricting in their intent or intelligent application. Since man's nature leads him to search endlessly for new accommodations,

> there is no possibility for maintaining a *status quo*. Even if we had enough learning and wisdom to achieve at any given time a harmonious state of ecological equilibrium..., it would be a dynamic equilibrium, which would be compatible with man's continuing development.[10]

Community is progressive, building a social legacy for the use of succeeding generations. The mandates recognize its volatile character, and give man a persisting obligation within which to exercise his growing comprehension and improved technology.

* * *

We have considered the significance of Jesus' lordship in its textual setting, and for subsequent time as realized through God's pattern for society. We shall next want to explore how it provides direction for (gives content to) those observing the mandate structure for community.

Bonhoeffer makes a valuable distinction in this connection: "Christ as idea is timeless truth; the idea of God embodied in Jesus is accessible to any one at any time. The word as address stands in contrast to this... . It is not timeless, but takes place in history."[11] Christ as *idea* is timeless truth. That is, Jesus revealed once and for all the eternal nature of God: His attributes and moreover His person.

What then of the Word as address? Bonhoeffer claims that where the Word as idea is timeless, the Word as address is timely. That is, it is experiential, the confrontation with Christ in terms of concrete responsibility.

The ideal needs first be explored. You can go about conserving in the wrong way. As a child, I spent countless hours playing with my soldiers, and for years the survivors were hidden away in boxes in the attic. One day they were discovered and resurrected for our children's use. The former fosters sentimentality, but the latter renders a service.

Some in a manner of speaking put Christ in a box and for all intent and purpose He remains there except for special occasions such as for attending church services. Then He is celebrated, not as a militant leader but a nostalgic figure from the past. This results in creedalism--strict conformity to conventional beliefs, and legalism--strict conformity to traditional ways. Whereas the old beliefs may be correct, and the old ways contain much wisdom, our legacy was meant to be proved in life's crucible rather than packaged away for sentimental reflection. The church was meant to be a mighty army rather than a museum.

The polar alternative serves no better: a radical contextualism loses needed perspective. All of us have had the experience of coming in on a discussion already in progress, and where no one makes the effort to fill us in. We sit there wondering how to interpret this or that observation, why a certain emotion is expressed, and what may be the point of some given interchange. Perhaps we make what seems an appropriate comment only to find that it is ignored or for no apparent reason rejected. The problem is that we lack the necessary historical background.

This is analogous to those striving for community without a constructive context. It results in existential humanism, a radical commitment to the present as immediately perceived. While in some ways commendable, it lacks a more comprehensive understanding required to achieve success.

What does Jesus offer as an alternative to an irresponsible celebration of the past or superficial crusade for the present? Guidance through the written Word.

Man speaks in order to communicate; he listens to others and in this way comprehends. Perhaps God could devise some other avenue for communication, but it is not clear what this would be. Words would seem to be the way to go.

Albert Schweitzer elaborates as follows: "Every saying contains in its own way the whole Jesus. The very strangeness and unconditionedness in which He stands before us makes it easier for individuals to find their own personal standpoint in regard to Him."[12] Schweitzer insisted on his thesis in defense of the apocalyptic figure he discovered in Scripture, and to rebuke others who felt free to alter what they read concerning Him.

Alan Stibbs reaches a similar conclusion. "For the written word is but the completion or reflection of the Living Word," he reasons. "It is, so to speak, the halo round His head in which His glory finds visible or intelligible, because verbal, expression."[13]

Once we have allowed Scripture to define Jesus as it would, we are in the enviable position of fine-tuning our relationship. First, He is the *wise* Other. We engage Him as incarnate Wisdom. Such sage advice as others may give suffers in comparison.

Second, He is the *reconciling* Other. "Here Christ stands, in the centre, between me and myself, between the old existence and the new."[14] He recovers me; He brings me to myself; He restores me to His way. The human analogy will have to suffice, since we have none better. We recall someone who was available at an opportune time, with insight into the dilemma we faced, communicating confidence, and offering constructive guidance. Although we continue to feel deeply indebted, life goes on.

Conversely, Jesus meets us time and again with a futurity that is present.   Wolfhart Pannenberg pointedly comments: "To love the preliminary (Jesus) is no little thing. Christians are surely right to call for devotion to Jesus. He who despises the preliminary because he waits for the ultimate will not be able to recognize the ultimate in its coming."[15] God's future is open to those acting now in faith. What will eventuate in time will not circumvent God's present provision. Christ is the door to life and all that life has to hold.

Third, Jesus is the *redeeming* Other. We experience His will as other and yet our own. Paul put it this way: "I have been crucified with Christ; and it is no longer I who live, but Christ lives in me; and the life which I now live in the flesh I live by faith in the Son of God, who loved me, and delivered Himself up for me" (Gal. 2:20). While Christ's will was becoming his, I suspect that every compatibility opened new areas of disparity. The Christian experience is like that, if we are honest with ourselves and others.

Christ's ministry results in the fruit of the Spirit. Paul contrasts the unifying ministry of love (Gal. 5:22) to the disintegrating influence of the works of the flesh (Gal. 5:20-21). (The former is like a balm for the many afflictions with which we are tormented.) He similarly contrasts the constructive result of power, love, and self-control to the disabling attack of fearful timidity (2 Tim. 1:7). Christ is not satisfied with our believing who He is, but in our becoming what He desires for us.

Life, for the Christian turns out to be an expanding experience of responsibility to and provision from God. It is community, located in the sovereignty of God, mediated by Christ, and actualized through the Holy Spirit. The disciple lives in a future reality already in a profound sense present. There are many things that he does not know, but he knows in Whom he believes, and commits his life to Christ's sustaining grace (2 Tim. 1:12). Then, and only then, can he confess with saints of all time that *Christ is Lord*!

Editorial note. As mentioned at the outset, these papers help fill in the gaps among various books published over the years. The above illustratively falls between *Psychology in the Psalms* (1969) and *Christianity Without Walls* (1972)/*Paced by God* (1973). While

Psychology in the Psalms dealt primarily with the existential nature of man, it introduced the social mandate theme picked up in this paper. The remaining two works were originally one manuscript, which I found necessary to separate for publication purposes. The first explored the vertical relationship of man, and the former his horizontal relationship in Christian community (an emphasis picked up in the article to follow).

ENDNOTES

1. William Ramsay, *The Christ of the Earliest Christians*, p. 32.
2. Joel Carmichael, *The Death of Jesus*, p. 133.
3. Dietrich Bonhoeffer, *Christianity*, p. 32.
4. Ramsay, *op. cit.*, p. 134.
5. Ibid., p. 54.
6. C.G. Montefiore, *Some Elements of the Religious Teaching of Jesus According to the Synoptic Gospels*, p. 57.
7. Vladimir Simkhovitch, *Toward an Understanding of Jesus*, p. 28.
8. Quoted from an unpublished document.
9. Samuel Schultz, *The Prophets Speak*, p. 47.
10. Rene Dubos, *So Human an Animal*, p. 264.
11. Bonhoeffer, *op. cit.*, p. 51.
12. Albert Schweitzer, *The Quest for the Historical Jesus*, p. 368. Schweitzer, as it would seem, fell prey to his own warning. His rejection of *consistent eschatology* derived from Scripture (as an interim consideration) in favor of the idea of reverence for life amounted to rejecting the Biblical norm.
13. Alan Stibbs, *Understanding God's Word*, p. 32.
14. Bonhoeffer, *op. cit.*, p. 19.
15. Wolfhart Pannenberg, *Theology and the Kingdom of God*, p. 126.

BIBLIOGRAPHY

Bonhoeffer, Dietrich. *Christology*. London: Collins, 1966.

Carmichael, Joel. *The Death of Jesus*. London: Pelican, 1966.

Dubos, Rene. *So Human an Animal*. New York: Scribners, 1969.

Montefiori, C.G. *Some Elements of the Religious Teaching of Jesus According to the Synoptic Gospels*. London: Macmillan, 1910.

Pannenberg, Wolfhart. *Theology and the Kingdom of God*. Philadelphia: Westminster, 1969.

Schultz, Samuel. *The Prophets Speak*. New York: Harper & Row, 1968.

Schweitzer, Albert. *The Quest for the Historical Jesus*. London: Black, 1922.

Simkhovitch, Vladimir. *Toward an Understanding of Jesus*. New York: Macmillan, 1951.

Stibbs, Alan. *Understanding God's Word*. London: Intervarsity, 1950.

MATTHEW AND THE HOUSE-CHURCHES*

Sherman Johnson raises the rhetorical question: "But why did laymen and readers in the house-churches of the Graeco-Roman read Matthew so avidly?"[1] The reasons which he introduces seem to enjoy a broad consensus, viz., the completeness of the narrative, and its unique qualification for ecclesiastical purposes. It is especially the latter which Johnson singles out, illustrating how suitable Matthew's style is for church use.

Matthew does qualify for its completeness and church utility, but the question is whether there may be a more basic reason for its popularity. It is this possibility that we will subsequently pursue.

Determination

Consider first the structure of Matthew's gospel. It falls primarily into five sections, each terminated by a version of *when he had finished these words* (7:28; 11:1; 13:53; 19:1; 26:1). These pivotal references not only conclude the formal instruction, but introduce subsequent activity--often punctuated by dialogue.

Look at these teaching sections more carefully. They deal in succession with life in the new community, the work and behavior of the disciples, the mystery of the kingdom, excellence, and the consummation. Consider, further, how the life of Christ ties into these blocks of teaching. The first three sections precede periods of relative obscurity, popularity, and opposition. The fourth marks the point at which Jesus leads His followers away from the familiar confines of Galilee to Perea and Judea, and the last introduces the passion account.

There remains one segment: the introduction to Christ's life and ministry (1:1-4:25). While this may throw some off track, it provides a necessary bridge to what follows. Imagine that the first gospel began with 5:1. (For all intent and purposes, the teaching does in fact begin here.)

*Reprinted by permission of *The Evangelical Quarterly.*

We read: "And when he... ." Who is He? The introduction establishes, both in terms of His genealogical and circumstantial qualifications, Jesus' messianic credentials. All that follows proceeds with this conviction in place.

Henry Theissen concludes:

> Matthew wrote to encourage and confirm the persecuted Jewish Christians in their faith, to confute their opponents, and to prove to both that the Gospel was not a contradiction of the teachings of the Old Testament, but rather a fulfillment of the promises made to Abraham and to David.[2]

First in order, as relates to the gospel; second, as this ties back into the salvation history that preceded it.

So much for the historical perspective in general, but what of the factual detail in Matthew? Two considerations seem trenchant. The detail in Matthew, messianic introduction excepted, appears less labored than in Luke, and in some ways less than Mark--whereas John's apologetic agenda makes comparison difficult. On the other hand, Matthew handles the teaching sections much more favorably, suggesting that we are dealing with what is essentially a stylistic feature.

In summary, we have in Matthew five major pedagogical sections, each introducing the disciples to a new course of events, representing Christian faith as a messianic openness, a versatility born of commitment. The prime concern of the gospel, thus understood, is to inculcate such a perspective, and the reason for its ready acceptance that it uniquely suited the needs of persons in cultural transition. It remains to elaborate what this thesis might imply.

DESCRIPTION

For a passage that at face value seems so relatively straight-forward, the Sermon on the Mount has lent itself to a remarkable variety of interpretations. This may suggest that we are not focusing on the larger context.

To whom was the message addressed? Jesus saw the multitude and retired to the slope of a hill, where He assumed a teaching position and the disciples came to Him (5:1). Then, as He neared the conclusion of His comments, the multitude was amazed at the authoritative manner in which He taught (7:28-29). Dietrich Bonhoeffer cogently reconstructs the situation by noting that Jesus taught His disciples in the presence of the multitude. Otherwise put, while particularly suited to the disciples, "the aim is to bring *all* who hear it to decision and salvation"[1]

The sermon in general and beatitudes in particular establishes the course which Matthew will explore:

> They express divergence from the established norms of society, the cost of discipleship, and the consequent happiness. The principles which they convey were personified in Christ. The Beatitudes are but guidelines; one's relationship to Christ is the crux of the issue. They are not so much a list of things to do as aids to the compulsive obedience felt by the disciples. They were also words of comfort which would be so necessary for the difficult days that lay ahead for those first disciples--and which no disciples may avoid. The Beatitudes set the tone for the Christian life: they are the priorities which make life meaningful.[4]

What the disciples learned from Jesus, they came to expect of themselves. What subsequent readers derived, they too applied to their lives as the Christian faith increasingly penetrated the Graeco-Roman world.

Faith in Christ may be thought of as a cultural shock of divine proportion. Life in Christ stands over against the self-life. It does not accommodate to one person, or one culture, against any other; but with Christ affirming all that is right against all that is wrong.

As a result, the gospel appears as good news for those who embrace it, but bad news for those who ignore it. The light either shines brighter as we progress, or becomes less visible as we persist in the opposite direction. This, along with the above, strikingly paralleled the experience of those in the early house-church movement--as if hand in glove.

The second collection of Jesus' sayings introduces the disciples into the nature of their responsibilities, both concerning behavior and mission. They receive such instruction as:

> As you go, preach, saying "The kingdom of heaven is at hand."
> Heal the sick, raise the dead, cleanse the leapers, cast out demons; freely you received, freely give.
> Do not acquire gold, or silver, or copper for your money belts, or a bag for your journey, nor even two tunics, or sandals, or a staff; for the worker is worthy of his support.
> And into whatever city or village you enter, inquire who is worthy in it; and abide there until you go away.
> Behold, I send you as sheep in the midst of wolves; therefore be shrewd as serpents and innocent as doves.
> But when they deliver you up, do not become anxious about how or what you will speak; for it shall be given you in that hour what you are to speak.

> What I tell you in the darkness, speak in the light; and what you hear in
> your ear, proclaim upon the housetops (10:8-11, 19, 27).

With these and complementary words, Jesus primed those who had
decided to follow Him--regardless of circumstances.

Jesus on occasion employs the analogy of a flock of sheep to depict
His disciples. "The picture of a flock, taken alone, could imply
thoughtless, passive existence for the disciple, a serenity secured upon
surrender of our mind and activity, but Jesus refuses us that possibility.
He urges us to preach, not indiscriminately but to whom we are sent."[5]

They were to minister to the whole person. Some would be inclined
to minister to one's immediate physical and social needs, to the exclusion
of the eternal. Others would focus on the eternal to the exclusion of all
else. Neither alternative would be acceptable.

Christian ministry, thus understood, is inherently radical--not in its
departure from some given consensus, but in contrast to all. (As the
Japanese theologian Kazoh Kitamori would observe, not for originating
in the West--which it did not, but from heaven.) It results not simply from
trying to imitate Jesus, but engage life with Him. It is not replica but
relationship. Thus the Graeco-Roman believers understood their life and
mission, drawing upon Jewish sources to serve the great commission to
evangelize all nations.

As a matter of record, their labors bore fruit. Not long after the turn
of the century, Justin Martyr could boast:

> For there is not a single race of men, whether among barbarians or Greeks,
> or by whatever name they may be called, of those who live in wagons or
> are called nomads or herdsmen living in tents, among whom prayers and
> thanksgivings are not offered through the name of the crucified Jesus to
> the Father and Maker of all things.[6]

Such was the nature of their early success, and confidence for the future.

Jesus' third block of instruction developed the mystery of the kingdom,
and anticipated the opposition which was growing. The gospel both rends
and restores; it separates brother from brother and makes brothers out of
foreigners. The Spirit of God works in mysterious ways, shattering the
citadels of time in favor of the reaches of eternity.

Seemingly in exasperation, the disciples asked Jesus: "Why do you
speak to them in parables?" (13:10). While His teaching seemed to them
to *accentuate* the mystery, Jesus countered that it *reflected* the ministry.
There was a hardness of heart which, if penetrated, will not be by

overpowering assault but as an invitation to life abundant. God was working, but in subtle fashion.

We could speculate further. It was not simply that the gospel was received by some and rejected by others, but it collided with the entrenched power structure--both in Jesus' day and in the time of Matthew's readers. Opposition grew among those who felt their invested interests were threatened. This, in turn, created persecution of the Christians. Tacitus comments as follows:

> Christ, for whom the name was derived, had been put to death in the reign of Tiberius by the procurator Pontius Pilate. The deadly superstition, having been checked for a while, began to break out again, not only throughout Judaea, where this mischief first arose, but also at Rome, where from all sides all things scandalous and shameful meet and become fashionable. Therefore, at the beginning some were seized who made confessions; then, on their information a vast multitude was convicted, not so much of arson as of hatred of the human race.[6]

Many would die, but many more lived daily in threat of death. Rejection and retribution increasingly stalked the believers, as they learned how to live with these unwelcome companions. Upon reflection, they drew strength from Jesus' example. They also pondered His teaching concerning suffering, as they were called up to experience it in their own lives.

Matthew speaks to this situation in convincing terms. It is not surprising that persons should respond when facing similar circumstances, then or now.

The next, relatively abbreviated, teaching section revolves around the question of who is greatest in the kingdom, coming to focus on forgiveness and living a life free of offence (18:1f).

> There comes a transition from what had been such a grand vision of Christ to petty bickering over who should be greatest in His kingdom (18:1-14). "Who then," press the disciples, "is greatest in the kingdom of heaven?" ...The disciples were hushed in anticipation of how He might respond.[8]

Jesus looked around at His disciples. They could feel His eyes penetrating their defenses, as if to determine the most likely candidate. Who would it be? Still His eyes swept on, past the inner circle to the remaining disciples, and finally rested on a little child. "Whoever then humbles himself as this child," Jesus concluded, "he is the greatest in the kingdom of heaven" (18:4).

Humility contrasts to *pride*. Richard Halverson comments on the latter:

> There are two diametrically opposite directions pride can follow, two extreme views it can take. One is the obvious, the other more subtle and more insidious, therefore more deceptive. One is conceit, the other contempt... . Contempt for self is pride in reverse or the lack side of conceit.[9]

Humility looks past self toward service. It takes praise and criticism in stride, while in search for excellence. In the process, it returns good for evil.

> Humility, we conclude, remains the key to life, an honest examination of what it means to live in God's world and with those created in His image. And mutual concern is how humility fleshes itself out in practice, dealing realistically with but willing to forgive those offenses which inevitably result.[10]

The final instruction section deals with the end of the age, as it prepared the disciples for the passion experience (24:3; 26:2). Jesus' reply to the disciples' questions concerning the end time is an involved one: warning of the stresses of the time, the possibility of being misled, and the rigorous demands of discipleship. Then comes His contrast between *these things* (24:33)--which are pending, observable, and within their life time, and *that day and hour* (24:36)--which is expected, unpredictable, and in the Father's hand. That is surrender what you cannot save to gain what you cannot lose.

Perea was the least Jewish of the provinces at that time. Rub the surface anywhere and you would likely come up with paganism. This would prove to be a valuable training ground for the disciples' wider ministry to the nations.

Judea was saturated with religious instruction. Conservative by design, it would prove to be most resistant to change. The disciples had their work cut out for them.

No doubt they would have turned back were they simply concerned for the short run. It was as they kept their gaze fixed on the distant horizon that they could continue pressing ahead. As with the adage, it is darkest before the dawn.

Time was running out. "My Father," Jesus urgently prayed, "if it is not possible for this cup to pass away unless I drink it, may your will be done" (26:42). He was resolute to the end.

The disciples would have occasion to think back on Jesus' words. They would come to the end of human resolve, only to forge on enabled by God. This would be *their* passion experience. While not restricted to the martyrs, they perhaps best illustrate the phenomenon.

This *passion experience* might seem to fly in the face of logic. On the one hand, life may be freely surrendered; on the other, it takes on eternal significance. It results when God's will becomes so paramount that concern for others outweighs all else. It musters what little we have for a climactic expression of confidence. It can even remove the black crape from Good Friday.

The first-century house-churches were alive--alive to Christ, the reality of Christian fellowship, and the responsibilities for world conquest. They were rejoicing in the blessedness which transcended their circumstances, colored their ministry, and whetted their anticipation. In Matthew's gospel they found a text remarkably applicable to their situation. It helped them worship, will, and work. Its theme was messianic, and came across as dynamic, open, and unashamed. Perhaps written by Matthew with the Hebrew Christian especially in mind, it was in the providence of God certainly intended for all those passing through cultural transition--a moving message for a mobile people.

Editorial note. The above article was eventually expanded into a book length manuscript published as *Celebrating Jesus as Lord* (1974). The notion of *openness toward the future*, touched on in this context and others, becomes the prime focus in the next paper and final entry from this time frame.

ENDNOTES

1. *The Interpreter's Bible*, Vol. 7, p. 232.
2. Henry Thiessen, *Introduction to the New Testament*, p. 137.
3. Dietrich Bonhoeffer, *The Cost of Discipleship*, p. 119.
4. Morris Inch, *Psychology in the Psalms*, p. 67.
5. Morris Inch, *Celebrating Jesus as Lord,* pp. 38-39.
6. Justin Martyr, *Dialogue with Trypho*, p. 117.
7. Tacitus, *Annals*, XV, 44.
8. Inch, *Celebrating Jesus as Lord*, p. 73.
9. Richard Halverson, *Christian Maturity*, p. 121.
10. Inch, *Celebrating Jesus as Lord*, p. 80.

BIBLIOGRAPHY

Bonhoeffer, Dietrich. *The Cost of Discipleship*. New York: Macmillan, 1963.

Justin Martyr. *Dialogue with Trypho*.

Halverson, Richard. *Christian Maturity*. Los Angeles: Cowman, 1956.

Inch, Morris. *Celebrating Jesus as Lord*. Chicago: Moody, 1974.

_____. *Psychology in the Psalms*. Waco: Word, 1969.

The Interpreter's Bible (George Buttrick, ed.). 12 vols. Nashville: Abingdon-
  Cokesbury, 1951-1963.

Tacitus, *Annals*.

Thiessen, Henry. *Introduction to the New Testament*. Grand Rapids:
  Eerdmans, 1946.

THE TRANSCENDENCE OF GOD
AND AN OPEN FUTURE*

Harvey Cox developed contrasting perspectives concerning life from the story of *Chicken Licken*. You may recall that Chicken Licken concluded from an acorn rattling off his head that the sky was falling. Chicken Licken, Cox observes, was an apocalyptic chicken. That is, he was a farm-yard prophet of doom.

> An unqualified apocalypticism is nihilistic; all earthly goals are equally corrupt and illusory. One cannot think rationally about means since life is determined by irrational powers and malevolent forces. Rational action is useless because powers outside history and beyond human control will quickly bring the whole thing to a blazing end.[1]

It follows that the apocalyptic is anti-political, and it is in this vein that Susan Sontag interprets the film *Dr. Strangelove*:

> For *Doctor Strangelove* is not, in fact, a political film at all... . The end of *Dr. Strangelove,* with its matter-of-fact image of apocalypse and flip soundtrack ("We'll Meet Again"), reassures us in a curious way, for nihilism is our contemporary form of moral uplift. As *The Great Dictator* was Popular Front optimism for the masses, so *Doctor Strangelove* is nihilism for the masses, a philistine nihilism.[2]

Cox is similarly critical of the teleological perspective, illustrated by the resolute acorn lying in the dust where it has fallen. There is only one future for an acorn, to become an oak tree. There being no other alternatives, the irrationalism of the apocalyptic is replaced with by the irrevocability of cosmic purpose.

Teleological thinking puts its emphasis on the beginning, the *arche*.

*Reprinted in accordance with the automatic permission policy of *Christian Scholar's Review.*

The telos is really the highest development of the arche. The whole oak tree is there in the acorn and has but to develop and grow. Teleology projects onto history, which should be the realm of radical freedom and responsibility, a way of thinking derived from nature, which is the realm of development and necessity.[3]

Cox consequently concludes:

If nihilistic anti-politics is modern, secularized apocalypticism, then teleology is the nature religion: it makes man feel a little more at home in the bewildering cosmos, a little closer to plants, stars, and animals. But it has the same disadvantage. It obscures man's special character as a historical creature, as an animal with memory and hope who knows that if he destroys his world he can no longer blame it on forces beyond his control.[4]

The work of Teilhard de Chardin illustrates in a general way the teleological point of view. That is to say, he locates humanity in a purposeful cosmic order. Still, he goes beyond the teleological approach by suggesting that man uniquely holds the key to the next stage in the cosmic design, that what happens from now on is rather up to him. In this regard, Cox sees his teleology ripening into a third perspective, the prophetic.

Cox proceeds to describe the conflict between Yahweh and Baal as a cataclysmic contest between the teleological and prophetic.

It was a battle between two views of man. Was man totally enmeshed in nature, an expression to its vitalities and powers, or was man a historical creature, called by a God who acted in historical events and who required him to take responsibility for himself and his world on the way to an open future?[5]

Underscore the phrase *an open future*. What does it imply? It is a future open to man, a book for which he writes the chapters. Man cannot excuse himself as the result of random happening or fatalistic forces; the future is his to create. The point is perhaps unwittingly illustrated in Leroy Augenstein's *Come Let Us Play God.*[6] In this recent work, Augenstein delves into some of the possibilities for genetic control, and the ethical dilemma raised by modern advances. He thereby assumes human responsibility under the rubric of *playing God.*

Cox is, to be sure, putting down straw men. If one had an affinity for one of the positions discredited, he would still be reluctant to admit it. That is, the categories are loaded; only the prophetic is given in a favorable light. Since this would seem to be the case, it suggests that we take a second look at the options.

The key to the apocalyptic is the inscrutability of life. Can anyone doubt the ambiguity of existence? Who in his right mind clicks off pat answers to puzzling problems? And how many times a day do we catch ourselves asking: "Now, why did this or that happen?" John Ingalls posed the reluctance of life to surrender its answer with the observation: "Every cradle asks us, 'Whence?' and every coffin 'whither?' The poor barbarian, weeping over his dead, can answer these questions as intelligently as the robed priest of the most authentic creed" (*Address at a Little Boy's Grave*). True, we press ahead, picking up the pieces as we go. Birth is for the living, and burial for the dead, but the interim poses more questions than provides answers.

The apocalyptic, then, preserves the dimension of mystery. But beyond this, it protects the holy from desecration, by reserving an abode for God alone. This calls to mind a text that reads: "After these things I looked, and behold, a door standing open in heaven and the first voice which I heard, like a trumpet speaking with me, saying 'Come up here, and I will show you what must take place after these things'" (Rev. 4:1). Whereupon, John's attention was turned away from the internal struggles and external persecution of the churches, to ponder what God would bring to pass. Assured of God's benevolent intent, the veil would soon drop-- leaving the apostle to wrestle with the problems at hand.

Finally, the apocalyptic is not categorically in opposition to human accountability. Note the refrain to the churches: *he that overcomes* (2:7, 11, 17, 26; 3:5, 12, 21). Those who gain mastery over life realize the promises of God. His is no simple gift, but the grace to accept and exercise responsibilities.

The teleological also has something to be said for it. Elsewhere, I suggested that we add facticity to the consideration of freedom and fate: "By facticity is meant the sum total of determinants in any given situation. It includes not only those environmental factors external to man, but the physical and psychological makeup of the person. Facticity rescues freedom from fate, and fate from freedom."[7] Freedom and fate are mediated in connection with the conditions prevailing at the moment.

Moreover, the teleological perspective conserves the legacy of history; otherwise we would have to start from scratch each time around. We can build, each one upon the work of another, as Paul suggests: "I planted,

Apollos watered, but God was causing the growth" (1 Cor. 3:4). The apostle added to the interrelatedness of human activity God's enabling involvement. Perhaps the acorn is an unfortunate way of expressing God's effectual enterprise, but the reality nonetheless remains.

What are we to make of the discussion up to this point? It is that life is purposeful (teleological), imperfectly comprehended (apocalyptic), and in which man assumes an appropriate responsibility (prophetic). Each of the alternatives adds a needed ingredient to a comprehensive mix.

As a case in point, follow Moses to the wilderness by Horeb, where he encounters God (Exod. 3). "Here I am," Moses responded, using language with which he was familiar, as social legacy bequeathed by the teleological. At which, God instructed him to remove his sandals for the ground on which he stood was holy. Moses was a sandal-wearing, and I-know-what-holy-means person--further evidence of the teleological.

Even so, Moses was not surprisingly confounded by the experience. God revealed Himself as *I am*, as transcendent in His actuality. This provided no immediate point of contact, since the revelation was without specification, i.e., apocalyptic. In time, God would identify Himself in connection with Abraham, Isaac, and Jacob. This placed Moses in familiar surroundings, i.e., in teleological perspective. Then, just as he was feeling more secure, God mandated that he challenge Pharaoh. This amounted to a return to the apocalyptic with impending disaster. Forebodings aside, Moses embraced the prophetic role, initiated the exodus, and encouraged the Hebrew people to press on toward the promised land.

The prophetic role may be *playing God*, as Augenstein suggests, but it is decidedly not *being God*. In other words, process--yes, deification--no.

How is God transcendent? This is not a very good question. God simply is; it is not something or other that makes Him transcendent. It is not His groundness nor power which defines transcendence. It is His being, His actuality. Otherwise stated, it is His personhood. Cox criticizes this move for a reason I concur with, but will withhold comment for the present.

Friedrich Gogarten sets the stage for elaboration. Man, for Gogarten, is the creature in and for others. He finds himself in openness and availability. History results from community, the latter understood as the cooperative captivation of resistive forces.[8]

Where does God fit into the picture? God is the concealed Other, who meets us with ultimate obligation. He is the mystery of being reflected in the sense of corporate responsibility, to be in and for others and open to the unknown.

Gogarten adds an important qualification: God in Christ was man in and for others. From Christ we learn how man can act in response to God's initiatives, and realize that the failure to do so is sin. From Christ we learn to trust that the conditions of life are such that we can be with and for others, and open to the mystery of being.

Now, we return to pick up on Cox's complaint. He protests that thinking of God in personal terms may discourage social responsibility, and so it can. The pietistic alternative that settles for a warm heart while others are in need is both a distortion of the tradition and the Christian faith it seeks to nurture. But what I think Cox is insisting upon is that we properly qualify our theistic convictions. (When interviewed, he observed, tongue in cheek, that it is much too difficult to do an encore after announcing the demise of God.)

Qualification is in order. Gogarten's position would seem to lack particularity. Karl Barth, for instance, chides him for confusing God with the *volk*, the transcendent with the cultural. While his criticism appears well taken, God is not merely *wholly Other*--as Barth insists, but radically here. That is, whereas Gogargten's counter-charge that Barth's *wholly Other* is an irrelevant abstraction, while an overstatement, is not without merit.

"I believe in God the Father Almighty," reads the creed. God is. "Maker of heaven and earth," it continues. Man is.

Nevertheless, I am not in the same way God is; I am because He is. God is not only a clue to *numinous*, the experience of the Other, but to *ego*, the experience of self. We are accustomed to think that we are and that God might be, and develop elaborate arguments to *prove* the existence of God. The Biblical writers, however, do not move in that direction. They do not consider man and confess God, but confess God and consider man.

Barth and Gogartgen close ranks with the incarnation. The author of Hebrews concludes that God revealed Himself to us in the parade of prophets, culminating in the Christ (3:1). That is, there was a progressive revelation which cast light on the nature of God, and, in turn, on man. The two become superimposed with the advent of Christ. The *I am* was here.

We should consider further the dynamics of revelation. Each subsequent revelation might clarify or extend, but not reverse what was previously made known. It resembles a classroom in which the teacher lays down principles he intends to build upon.

Sometimes the truth of God was turned against the Almighty. Man tried to tie God to a time, place, or custom. He devised legalistic defenses to shield himself from the living God. Whereupon, God raised up a prophet to speak on His behalf. It was not His intent to constrict life unnecessarily, but to protect us from evil. He did not want to hold back His blessing, but bestow it when conditions warranted it.

Not all supposed revelations, to be sure, were true. How could one distinguish the true from the false? "Is it from God?" asked the seer. That is, was it consistent with the ideas and ideals previously expressed. "Does it come to pass?" he further inquired. That is, does it translate into reality.

Notwithstanding, there was the unexpected. For Moses, it was a burning bush, a solemn voice, and an ambassadorial call. We must anticipate that God will *surprise* us from time to time, as an evidence of His remarkable creativity. Then, in retrospect, you hear someone say: "It is just like Him to do something like that." So it is!

Jesus' prayer *not My will but Thine* reflects such confidence in God's creative design. One would not welcome the prospect of crucifixion. Another alternative would certainly be preferable. Even so, if this were God's way, the benefits would far outweigh the consequences.

Revelation, as implied earlier, is particularizing. It brings God better into focus by way of what it affirms and negates. God approves of this; He does not approve of that. A pattern begins to take form.

We soon discover that God's ways are not ours, as far as the heavens are removed from the earth. For this reason, the prophets go to great lengths to encourage us to disassociate ourselves from the prevailing practices of our time. Free yourself from conventional wisdom; open your life to what exciting possibilities God has in store for you.

It comes time to summarize and highlight our discussion to the present concerning God and an open future. Alfred North Whitehead is reported as saying: "God and the world interact and effect each other; the initial aim which God offers to successive entities is continually adjusted to allow for environmental changes, so to aim for maximum intensity of experience according to the circumstances of the moment."[10] That is, optimum openness results from cooperation with the self-revealing God, incorporating the apocalyptic, teleological, and prophetic dimensions of life. Openness respects the apocalyptic, as divine transcendence, and the mystery of God's ways (Isa. 55:8). Openness embodies the teleological as well, with the perseverance of divine purpose, turning even man's rebellion to serve God's ultimate goals.   Openness finally and emphatically projects the prophetic, with man responsible to exercise stewardship over what has been entrusted to him.

Revelation identifies the person and purpose of God, the nature and obligation of man, and the conditions for effective cooperation. Rather than restricting man's potential, revelation explores how we can realize it. Scripture is life's script, a story of divine and human interplay. If we perform on cue, both we and others benefit from our performance.

I much prefer the analogy of marriage to Cox's fragmented barnyard to consider the various options. Man bonded to God experiences the apocalyptic, teleological, and prophetic aspects of life as an increasingly demanding but enriched experience. The future is thereby maximally open to those who deem to walk to God. While it opens through a narrow gate, the way broadens the further we follow it. Conversely, those who take the broad way find that it becomes increasingly restrictive until they come to a dead end. All of this is by way of saying that we opt for a transcendent God and an open future, or for neither one.

Editorial note. This theme was further elucidated in *Paced by God* (1973). With this topic, the curtain falls on the *Sixties*, as we move our calenders ahead.

ENDNOTES

1. Harvey Cox, *On Not Leaving it to the Snake*, pp. 38-39.
2. Susan Sontag, *Against Interpretation*, p. 149.
3. Cox, *op. cit.*, p. 41.
4. Ibid.
5. Ibid.
6. Leroy Augenstein, *Come, Let Us Play God.*
7. Morris Inch, *Psychology in the Psalms*, p. 159.
8. Friedrich Gogarten, *Demythologizing and History and The Reality of Faith.*
9. Inch, *op. cit.*, p. 13.
10. Lucien Price, *Dialogues of Alfred North Whitehead*, p. 160.

BIBLIOGRAPHY

Augenstein, Leroy. *Come Let Us Play God.* New York: Harper & Row, 1969.

Cox, Harvey. *On Not Leaving It to the Snake.* New York: Macmillan, 1967.

Gogarten, Friedrich. *Demythologizing and History.* London: SCM, 1955.

_____. *The Reality of Faith.* Philadelphia: Westminster, 1959.

Inch, Morris. *Psychology in the Psalms.* Waco: Word, 1969.

Price, Lucien. *Dialogues of Alfred North Whitehead.* Boston: Little, Brown, 1956.

Sontag, Susan. *Against Interpretation.* New York: Farrar, Straus, and Giroux, 1966.

INTO THE *EIGHTIES*

1986 was for me a pivotal year. It brought to a close virtually a quarter of a century of teaching at Wheaton College, and opened up new and exciting opportunities abroad.

As representative of the earlier phase, I have included three rather distinctive papers in this section. They probe the issues of religious authority, denominational diversity, and an understanding of myth. Considered separately and in order, they offer a reasoned approach to the Biblical foundation for Christian dogma, alternative ways of understanding the proliferation of diverse faith groups, and an exploration into the character of *God-talk*. Taken together, these papers further refine our comprehension of man searching for his place in God's world.

An Evangelical Approach to Biblical Authority was originally presented at a consultation of Lutheran and Evangelical theologians, and subsequently published in *The Covenant Quarterly*. *Reappraisal of Denominationalism* was read at an annual meeting of the American Academy of Religion. *Myth in Theological Discourse* was introduced at a gathering of the *Evangelical Theological Society*.

AN EVANGELICAL APPROACH TO BIBLICAL AUTHORITY*

We cannot speak of *the* Evangelical approach to Biblical authority as if the Evangelical movement were monolithic or its perspectives on the authority of Scripture were uniform. I shall discuss *an* Evangelical approach, namely one which is compatible with the Wheaton confessional statement: its immediate historical antecedent (particularly the *old Princeton tradition*), and the current campus theological mind-set. It also sacrifices the rich diversity in the Wheaton community in order to articulate a corporate perception.

Historical/Theological Setting

The current Wheaton doctrinal statement was adopted in 1926 (the college having begun in 1860 with the assets realized from a preparatory school established in 1852 on the present site) and has been refined in some regards with the passing of time. Its preamble explains that the document provides a summary of Biblical doctrine "that is consonant with evangelical Christianity. The statement accordingly reaffirms salient features of the historic creeds, thereby identifying the College not only with the Scripture but also with the Reformers and the evangelical movement of recent years." William Hodern correctly identifies the agenda of those in this tradition when he observes that "their primary interest was in defense of orthodox Christianity."[1] *Orthodox Christianity*, as used in this context, implies such faith as has generally characterized those who profess the Christian faith, and as expressed in the traditional creeds.

More specifically, the modern Evangelical movement set its defense of Christian orthodoxy against what it perceived to be an improper accommodation to the Enlightenment. Thus we understand the words of the Princeton divine, J. Gresham Machen, when he affirmed that

*Reprinted by permission of *The Covenant Quarterly.*

the present time is a time of conflict; the great redemptive religion which has always been known as Christianity is battling against a type of religious belief, which is only the more destructive of the Christian faith because it makes us of traditional terminology.[2]

The conflict was for him between Christianity rightly understood and *modern naturalistic liberalism.*

The Wheaton statement on Biblical authority reads: "We believe in the Scriptures of the Old and New Testaments as verbally inspired by God and inerrant in the original writing, and that they are of supreme and final authority in faith and life."

Commentary

The remainder of the paper will be a commentary on the article in the Wheaton statement, with special reference to the relationship between the authority of Christ and that of Scripture. The article on Biblical authority is the first of nine articles, the subsequent ones dealing with the nature of God, Christ, man, the atonement, exaltation of Christ, *the blessed hope,* regeneration, and the eternal state. Hodern observes that "to meet the challenge to orthodoxy--these men chose to make the doctrine of the errorless Bible the first line of defense."[4] While this comment makes it sound as if it were a strictly arbitrary decision based on the effort to achieve a strategic advantage, this was seldom, if ever, the way it was viewed by those espousing the position. They were inclined to represent what has been described as a *high view* of Biblical authority as a theological corollary to the nature of Scripture as the Word of God and consistent with the textual phenomena.

In the Scriptures of the Old and New Testaments

There are according to John Stott, in an address on Biblical authority before a Wheaton audience, two fundamental questions that religion must confront: by what authority we believe what we believe and how man may be reconciled to God. The subject of Biblical authority is therefore no trivial matter but of critical and fundamental importance.

There have been three basic views in regard to authority: reason, tradition, and Scripture. Some believe because the matter appeals to their understanding or a general consensus of those with whom they freely identify. Others believe because it is what the church teaches. Still others believe on the basis of Biblical teaching, and this last position suits the Evangelical thinking. It supposes that where reason and tradition are the words of men, no matter how true they may be, the Scripture alone qualifies as the infallible Word of God. That is not to say that Evangelicals despise either reason or tradition, for these contribute to their understanding of Scripture and its application to life.

We come then to the heart of the Evangelicals' commitment to Biblical authority: they take their stand out of loyalty to Christ. It is in response to Jesus' example and in keeping with His instruction. It assumes Jesus' prerogative with this topic as well as any other. If Jesus is Lord, we cannot pick and choose which teaching we will embrace.

How did Jesus regard the Old Testament Scripture? Stott develops an answer in three connections: as to His conduct, in His ministry, and concerning His controversies. Jesus when tempted in the wilderness responded time and again: "It is written" (Matt. 4:4, 6, 10). Stott reminisces that he used to think that Jesus was "throwing Scripture at Satan," but this was not the case. Jesus was instead telling Satan what *He* would do, in His behavior and out of deference to the authority of Scripture. He thus observed its authority through His conduct.

Jesus also accepted the authority of Scripture for His ministry. He announced His strategy in the synagogue at Nazareth with the words taken from Isaiah:

> The Spirit of the Lord is on me,
> because he has anointed me to preach good news to the poor.
> He has sent me to proclaim freedom for the prisoners
> and recovery of sight for the blind,
> to release the oppressed,
> to proclaim the year of the Lord's favor (Luke 4:18-19).

He exercised this ministry, as subsequent events would testify, in accordance with Scripture.

Jesus likewise referred to the authority of Scripture in His controversies. He inquired of the Sadducees: "Are you not in error because you do not know the Scriptures or the power of God?" (Mark 12:24). He also objected to the practice of the Pharisees in breaking God's command for the sake of their traditions.

> For God said, "Honor your father and mother" and "Anyone who curses his father or mother must be put to death." But you say that if a man says to his father or mother,'"Whatever help you might otherwise have received from me is a gift devoted to God, he is not to honor his father with it. Thus you nullify the word of God for the sake of your tradition" (Matt. 15:4-6).

Jesus thereby pressed His adversaries with an appeal to the authority of Scripture.

There remains to consider how the New Testament fits into the picture. We believe that Jesus intended and made provision for the New Testament Scripture. Jesus spoke to His disciples: "I have much more to say to you, more than you can bear. But when he, the Spirit of truth comes, he will guide you into all truth. He will not speak on his own; he will speak only what he hears, and he will tell you what is yet to come" (John 16:12-13). Now what Jesus promised was intended primarily for the apostles and only in a derived sense for us. In this way, He made provision for the New Testament and suggested the apostles' role in that regard.

An *apostle* is one sent to speak on behalf of another. It is as if the one who sends is the one who speaks. In such a manner, the apostle spoke God's word.

We are assured of this conclusion by the way the apostles understood their role, the authentication of their ministry through signs and wonders, and the recognition of the early Christians. Paul wrote to the Galatians: "Even though my illness was a trial to you, you did not treat me with contempt or scorn. Instead, you welcomed me as if I were an angel of God, as if I were Christ Jesus himself" (Gal. 4:14). The apostle did not protest as if to argue that they should have behaved differently, but took it as a recognition of his calling.

The apostolic office was further attested by signs and wonders accompanying the ministry. We read that "many wonders and miraculous signs were done by the apostles" (Acts 2:43), and again, "The apostles performed many miraculous signs and wonders among the people" (Acts 5:12). The book of Acts may be thought of as the acts of the apostles, so evidenced by the extraordinary results of their ministry.

The apostolic office was finally recognized as such by the early Christians. Ignatius consequently confessed: "I speak not to you as an apostle, but as a sinner and a condemned man." Stott thereupon sets aside the notion of apostolic succession in favor of apostolic doctrine and fellowship. We thus rely on the Scripture as our directive in matters of faith and practice, and understand this as generated out of loyalty to Christ. If Jesus exhibits and admonishes a high regard for the Scripture, we would expect to do no less.

As a result, we conclude that to hold to Biblical authority is not an Evangelical idiosyncrasy but *Christian*. It is to assure His lordship concerning Scripture as we would in other matters of faith.

Do we have problems with this article of faith? Certainly there are problems. What do we do with the problems? We wrestle with them, but we do not give up on what we believe Jesus practiced and taught.

Consider our belief in the living character of God as an example. Does that create difficulties for us? Of course it does. We see innocents suffering, the birth of a child with mental defects, or the random destruction of a tornado testing our confidence. Even so, we do not give up on God's love, anymore that Jesus did. In like manner, we hold firmly to the unqualified authority of Scripture. It is no less our faith for being a troubled faith. It is in fact such testing that distinguishes genuine faith from credulity.

We must remind ourselves that if we as Evangelicals hold to such a view of Scripture, this should be borne out in our approach to it. If we believe in its teaching and dependability, we should commit ourselves to a lifelong study of its text; if we believe, we ought to acknowledge its promises; if we believe, we ought to obey its commands; if we believe, we ought to communicate its message. As Jesus lived in accordance with Biblical authority, so ought those who bear His name as *Christians*.

Stott's discussion in effect lifts the authority issue out of the realm of Biblical criticism, and attaches it to Christology. Biblical criticism no longer can serve as a disguise for an Enlightenment's repudiation of Christianity or conversely a straw man for the apologist's harangue. It rather becomes a tool to further our understanding instead of a polemic device in theological disputation.

Gordon Fee pertinently observes: "The point is that not every Biblical statement is the word of God in precisely the same way."[5] He consequently recognizes a rich array of literary and historical data that contribute to our appreciation of the authoritative Word of God. He thereupon warns against certain unexamined presuppositions and unacceptable applications of Biblical criticism.

As verbally inspired by God and inerrant in the original writing

We recall the intent of the statement from its preamble, that it identify the college "not only with the Scriptures but also with the Reformers and the evangelical movement of recent years." Nowhere is the purpose of relating to the Evangelical movement more clearly expressed than in terms of verbal inspiration and inerrancy as regards the original writing. The term *inerrancy* came into vogue as a means to affirm a high regard for Biblical authority, consistent with that of traditional Christianity, unshaken by the subsequent impact of Enlightenment thought. It was not thought of as a new innovation, but a means of giving concrete expression to a traditional conviction.

Even so, Jack Rogers and Donald McKim describe the historical context as follows:

> The Princeton theologians felt that a firmly secured Scripture was needed. In the face of critical studies and new scientific *facts*, the Bible now had to be defended in a new way. Princeton saw it as imperative to defend the Scriptures as scientifically *errorless* documents. A.A. Hodge therefore found it necessary to clarify and rigidify the Princeton doctrine. Hence in 1789 he asserted that only the original autographs of the Scriptures were verbally inerrent.[6]

One can sense in this quotation not only the drift of the authors' thinking but something of their strident attitude toward the old Princeton tradition.

While Rogers and McKim's reconstruction has been subject to criticism, we ought not to allow the controversy to obscure the need for continuing theological reflection. No simple reference to the past can suffice to resolve the subsequent issues raised in the exercise of historical-critical methods.

The associated references to verbal inspiration and the original writings should consequently be appreciated within their historical setting and for the purpose they were intended. The idea of verbal inerrancy suggests that we understand the Scriptures as not simply a record of God's mighty acts but His own privileged interpretation of the meaning of those acts. (The exodus or resurrection might be interpreted in almost limitless fashion but for the fact that Scripture provides a normative explanation.) We are not free to revise Biblical teaching to accommodate our contemporary preference. The Scripture does not err in its inspired commentary.

The reference to original writings was a polemic device meant to assert what cannot be demonstrated but seemed appropriate from the Biblical data. There are textual problems, as Machen and his associates recognized, but it did not seem to them that these warranted the kind of skepticism promoted by their protagonists, let alone the alternatives promoted as a result. It rather appeared that their theological opposition had built a superstructure of insinuation and conjecture upon an inadequate foundation of hard-core textual problems. Such difficulties as exist might and likely should be explained on the basis of textual transmission.

Of supreme and final authority in faith and life

While the previous comment appears intended to tie the Wheaton statement into "the evangelical movement of recent years," the final reference to authority in faith and life is more reminiscent of Reformation rhetoric. Bernard Ramm observes that "Although evangelicals have differences within their own household, they are almost in uniform agreement with the Reformer's theological stance."[7]

The most favorable light in which to view Rogers and McKim's posturing would be to portray it as an effort to recover a broader based Evangelical consensus with the Reformation, and thereby escape some of the infighting of more recent times. At worst, it downplays the pressing issue of Biblical authority with which Evangelicals have concerned themselves.

In any case, the ultimate question is, as Stott reminds us, whether we express a confidence concerning Scripture consistent with our confession that Jesus is Lord. This, in turn, involves not merely what we think about Scripture, but how we revere its teachings, accept its promises, and act upon its injunctions. We cannot hope to be obedient to Jesus, and treat lightly the text He cherished.

Furthermore, the Evangelical attitude ought not promote its tradition uncritically, but to stir up one another to take the Scripture with all seriousness as the prized revelation of God to man. It must covet the hope of becoming better disciples of Christ and hence worthy of the designation *people of the book.*

Editorial note. Whereas the earlier papers turned our attention toward the Jesus paradigm in hopes of gaining better self-understanding, the above insists on the importance of taking up this quest in deference to Biblical authority. It decidedly takes issue with those who would set Jesus over against Scripture in an adversarial role. Even so, we may construct different traditions, as illustrated by the next topic concerning the proliferation of denominations.

ENDNOTES

1. William Hodern, *A Layman's Guide to Protestant Theology*, p. 57.
2. J. Gresham Machen, *Christianity and Liberalism*, p. 2.
3. Charles Blanchard, second president of Wheaton College, was on the drafting conference of the World Christian Fundamentalist Association, and subsequently introduced the confession of faith.
4. Hodern, *op. cit.*, p. 57.
5. Gordon Fee, "The Genre of the New Testament Literature and Biblical Hermeneutics," *Interpreting the Word of God* (Schultz and Inch, eds.), p. 105.
6. Jack Rogers and Donald McKim, *The Authority and Interpretation of the Bible*, p. 308.
7. Bernard Ramm, *The Evangelical Heritage*, p. 38.

BIBLIOGRAPHY

Fee, Gordon. "The Genre of the New Testament Literature and Biblical Hermeneutics," *Interpreting the Word of God* (Schultz and Inch, eds.), pp. 105-127.

Hodern, William. *A Layman's Guide to Protestant Theology*. New York: Macmillan, 1955.

Machen, J. Gresham. *Christianity and Liberalism*. Grand Rapids: Eerdmans, 1923.

Ramm, Bernard. *The Evangelical Heritage*. Waco: Word, 1973.

Rogers, Jack and Donald McKim. *The Authority and Interpretation of the Bible*. New York: Harper & Row, 1979.

Schultz, Samuel and Morris Inch (eds.). *Interpreting the Word of God*. Chicago: Moody, 1976.

A REAPPRAISAL OF DENOMINATIONALISM

This is in the character of an occasional paper, a spin-off study in the area of ethno-theology. It was also provoked by interaction with adherents of the so-called *Local Church*, which repudiates denominationalism as a denial of the unity of the Christian fellowship. The former resembles the steady flow of a river, and the latter some small tributary momentarily cresting from a cloud-burst and expelling its contents.

Theoretical Constructs

We shall first consider several of the classic theories of denominationalism, and then propose an alternative. We ought to think of these options as vantage points, some better than others, from which to view the subject. They are not strictly speaking exclusive of one another, except as they offer a distinctive perspective on the topic.

First, we consider Christopher Dawson's thesis. He views denominations as the tragic result of the collapse of *Christendom*, the western political and social establishment of Christianity. He consequently reasons that

> the tragedy of schism is that it is a progressive evil. Schism breeds division, until every social antagonism is reflected in some new religious division and no common Christian culture is conceivable. In the old world of united Christendom these social antagonisms were as strong as they are today, but they were antagonisms within a common society, and the Church was seen as the ultimate bond of unity.[1]

What has changed is not the intensity of antagonism, but loss of the ultimate bond of unity, resulting in the proliferation of denominations.

Dawson proposes a tension between *authority* and *reformation* within the church, a necessary tension which in this instance broke down with the Protestant revolt. He elaborates as follows:

> Protestant Reformation of the 16th century represents a final breach between the Papacy and the Northern Reformers--between the principle of authority and the principle of reformation. Both principles were alike essential to the traditions of Western Christendom, and even in the state of division neither part of the Christian world could dispense with them. Therefore, the Catholic world developed a new reforming movement, as represented by the Jesuits and the other new religious orders; while the Protestant world had to create new patterns of authority and theological tradition, such as we see in the ecclesiastical disciplines of the Calvinist Churches.[2]

The Reformation, thus conceived, resulted from the error of separating those principles which were meant to be kept in juxtaposition, and uncritically advocating one against the other.

The conflict between partisan supporters of authority and reformation left the terrain undefended against the incursion of secularism. Dawson presses his rationale with the observation that it was during the time of this

> sterile and inclusive religious conflict that the ground was prepared for the secularization of European culture. The convinced secularists were an infinitesimal minority of the European population, but they had no need to be strong since the Christians did their work for them.[3]

The secularists consequently moved in to possess the inheritance wasted by religious warfare.

Denominationalism, from this perspective, represents the effort to recover the authority-reformation tension but within a restricted domain. The over-arching unity was lost, as well as its infusion into a political and social establishment. We have thereby entered upon the era of denominationalism with the collapse of Christendom.

While Dawson seems to offer no hope except for a prodigal's return to *Mother Church*, this would seem to ignore the genius of his thesis. We assuredly cannot proceed as if nothing has happened. It would be more realistic to incorporate developments within long range goals, learning from the past but pressing on into a more promising future. In particular, Dawson's model implies an ecumenical ideal, and this ideal might take some creative turn. If so, we may benefit from the varied traditions then restored in a dynamic tension within a corporate fellowship.

Second, we turn to H. Richard Niebuhr's perspective on denominationalism as a religious sanction to social structure. He allows

> that it should not be true to affirm that the denominations are not religious groups with religious purposes, but it is true that they represent the accommodation of religion to the caste system. They are emblems, therefore, of the victory of the world over the Church, of the secularization of Christianity, of the Church's sanction of that divisiveness which the Church's gospel condemns.[4]

So while Niebuhr recognizes a mixed motivation, he deliberately accents social accommodation as a preeminent feature of the denominational dynamic. It is, as he graphically puts it, *the victory of the world over the church.*

Niebuhr goes on to castigate denominationalism as "the moral failure of Christianity. And unless the ethics of brotherhood can gain the victory over the divisiveness within the body of Christ it is useless to expect it to be victorious in the world."[5] Moreover, before we can hope to overcome such divisions as render the church ineffective, we must acknowledge the secular dimension of denominations.

Has denominationalism some redeeming ingredient? It would appear so since

> the rise of new sects to champion the uncompromising ethics of Jesus and "to preach the gospel to the poor" has again and again been the effective means of recalling Christendom to its mission. This phase of denominational history must be regarded as helpful, despite the break in unity which it brings about. The evil of denominationalism lies in the conditions which make the use of sects desirable and necessary: in the failure of the churches to transcend the social conditions which fashion them into caste-organizations... .[6]

Niebuhr thus pushes the fault back earlier, before the rise of the denominations, with a social accommodation that invites the former by way of protest. In the same breath, he acknowledges that the denominations fall prey to the same abuse they seek to alleviate through division.

He further suggests that a major reason for this accommodation is the church's concern for survival. It therefore forms an unholy alliance with the world in order to assure its own safety. It all too readily forgets that its strength resides not in alliance with the world, but uncompromising allegiance to the Almighty.

Niebuhr especially singles out for reproach the ecclesiastical compromise with an economic caste mentality. He observes in this connection that "the divisions of the church have been occasioned more frequently by the direct and indirect operation of economic factors than by the influence of any other major interest of man."[7] He adds that the economic factor not only initiates but often perpetuates divisions brought into being as a result of some other concern--such as with race.

While the economic accommodation is more subtle among the middle and upper than lower economic classes, it is no less present. Religion steps in to sanction wealth and excuse the lack of generosity. We have riches, according to this way of thinking, because we deserve it. Others lack because they are indolent or waste their opportunities.

Niebuhr does not leave in doubt what he sees as the resolution to this dilemma.

> For the proclamation of this Christianity of Christ and the Gospels a church is needed which has transcended the division of the world and has adjusted itself not to the local interests and needs of classes, races, or nations but to the common interests of mankind and the constitution of the unrealized kingdom of God.[8]

He thereby appeals for a genuinely universal church to rise above partisan rationalizations.

We note in passing that Dawson and Niebuhr's approaches follow a logical extension of their respective Roman Catholic and Protestant traditions. The former is more disposed to restrain the proliferation of denominations; the latter more open to seeing them as *desirable and necessary*. Both alike aspire to a more comprehensive expression of Christian unity.

Third, we entertain Winthrop Hudson's alternative. Hudson reports an ideological shift as instrumental in the rise of denominations. What we refer to as the *denominational* church concept was set forth a century earlier by the "Dissenting Brethren of the Westminster Assembly of Divines. The concept was to be of decisive future importance in the shaping of American religious life. Denominationalism, as these men used the term, was the opposite of sectarianism."[9]

Hudson proceeds to spell out the distinction:

> A *sect* regards itself alone as the true Church. By definition a *sect* is exclusive. *Denominationalism*, on the other hand, was adopted as a neutral and inclusive term. It implied that the group referred to is but one

member, called or denominated by a particular name, of a large group--the Church--to which other denominations belong.[10]

The denominations, thus understood, constitute no threat to church unity, but are rather advocates--assuming a less pretentious role within the total fellowship. Whether they fall short of the ideal is not the point at issue, but the ideal itself. It sets a course through denominationalism to a renewal of ecumenicity.

Hudson speaks without equivocation:

> On the basis of this understanding of the church which acknowledged the unity that existed within the diversity of outward ecclesiastical forms, the Protestant churches were able to develop a functional catholicity which was to find expression in the creation of a whole system of voluntary societies for the promotion of worthy causes. These were societies devoted to missions, Bible and tract distribution, education, charitable enterprises, and a wide-ranging spectrum of moral and social reforms.[11]

The key to this line of reasoning is *functional catholicity*. Our genuine unity is found in function rather than explicit form.

With this, we need to sort out some of the subtle nuances of this latest option. Hans Kung suggests that *ekklesia* is so complex a concept that we would do well to employ three translations: congregation, community, and church. He nonetheless concludes that the "three words are not in competition, but complement one another in translating the very rich and many-faceted *ecclesia.*"[12]

Kung advocates the use of *congregation* concerning the informal and unpredictable expression of Christian community. It suggests an affinity among Christians that draws them together, often in some quite unexpected fashion. This is primarily, although not exclusively, what Judson appears to have in mind as *functional catholicity*.

Kung reserves *community* for the institutional expression of the church, what some refer to as *the visible church*. This has to do with church order, ritual, and discipline: and may be extended to incorporate other features. It pertains to what Christians agree to do together as the people of God, and out of fidelity to His instruction and promise. It focuses primarily on the local fellowship.

This leaves the *church* designation to embrace the universal community of faith: past, present, and future. It would seem that Dawson and Niebuhr allow this church dimension to dominate their thinking, while Hudson directs his attention more to *congregation*.

In any case, Hudson has greatly relieved us of the burden associated with denominationalism. He sees it as opening the Christian fellowship to catholic renewal by way of an uninhibited response to the moving of God's Spirit. He unceremoniously shifts the emphasis from *being* to *act*, from concern over form to emphasis on function.

Finally, we consider Sidney Mead's contribution. He picks up the topic with the proliferation of American denominations:

> Religious freedom and the *frontier* provided the broad ideological and geographical setting in which these developments took place. This first meant the removal of traditional civil and ecclesiastical restrictions on vocal and organizational expressions of the religious convictions and even the whimsies of all men. The *frontier* provided the necessary space and opportunities in which such expressions could thrive.[13]

We should therefore understand denominationalism not in connection with opportunity alone or disposition alone, but the two taken together.

Mead explains that his

> general interpretation is based upon the view that what individuals and groups do when given freedom depends upon what they are (their character) when such freedom is offered. Hence an understanding of the development of what we note as characteristic traits of the denominations that took place during the formative period, hinges in large part upon a delineation of characteristic attitudes and practices that come to be accepted during the Colonial period.[14]

Mead elaborates his point of view concerning the disposition to conform more closely to the early church as set forth in the New Testament, character of American voluntarism, mission enterprise, revivalism, reaction against the Enlightenment stress on reason, and competition between the denominations.[15] This mix of concerns, when given the opportunity to express itself, resulted in the multiplication of denominations.

Mead attempts to hold the course of an objective observer. He appears reluctant to credit or discredit the spread of denominations. He rather seeks to understand the phenomenon as an aspect of social awareness.

What seems especially striking about his analysis is its stress on the internal ideological ferment which gives rise to denominations. He allows that the occasion must also be present, but this receives relatively little attention. It is rather the ideological mix that he scrutinizes with care. Herein, we discover the primary source and inventive design of the denominational endeavor.

We ought not overlook that the specific mixture he discovers is a blend of restoration to a more traditional faith and means of giving expression to some distinctive features of American culture. It, as a result, creates a new synthesis; which, hopefully, proves to be more faithful to the past and more relevant for the present. It sets aside in the process those previous efforts that no longer serve the purpose for which they were introduced. This results in a curious bifurcation that illustrates the complex nature of a denomination dynamic.

We have touched on four classic interpretations of the denominational phenomenon: the collapse of Christendom theory of Christopher Dawson, the social rationalism alternative of H. Richard Niebuhr, the confessional option of Winthrop Hudson, and the synthesis thesis of Sidney Mead. They reveal areas of consensus and conflict. All agree that denominationalism serves some need or combination of needs, although there is disagreement as to the character of need or how the denominations go about alleviating the need. All agree that the rise of denominations must be considered in connection with church unity, but each has a peculiar way of drawing the relationship. All agree that denominations can fail to achieve the purposes for which they were intended, but do not agree in their analysis of the dilemma or how to resolve it.

Further Proposal

It remains to develop an alternative that draws upon the previous options, but recasts them in a distinctive fashion. We shall designate this as a *contextualism* theory of denominationalism. It will employ concepts current in ethno-theological literature, along with other pertinent observations. We will cover the topic in a largely cursory fashion, which postpones detailed investigation to a later time.

We begin with what seems clear from the former studies: that denominations are, however else explained, an expression of contextual theology. Christians adopt their faith to meet some contemporary challenge. This may be primarily ecclesiastical, social, or political. As to whether it constitutes a threat to Christian unity, it depends on external circumstances and internal disposition.

While Dawson seems least willing to grant legitimacy to denominationalism, and Hudson most willing to do so, both stress its particular character--that which distinguishes one denomination from another. We see in these distinctive enterprises an effort to come to grips with life from a Christian perspective. They are, as such, cultural expressions.

The assumption that guides contextual theology is that the gospel can be faithfully expressed across cultural boundaries. Each respective culture provides a reasonable way of looking at life, once we come to understand what is involved. Some are more hospitable than others. None is immune from a Christian critique.

The ultimate success of Christian discipleship comes when persons *live the gospel back* within their own cultural orientation. Until such time, the gospel remains alien and inauthentic. Until such time, the gospel remains saddled with cultural baggage from the sending culture. Until such time, the Great Commission remains unfulfilled.

We hasten to add that without a sure hold on the authority of Scripture, contextualism results in a compromise of faith. As I have insisted on other occasions, whereas tradition and reason may be true--as the words of men, only the Scripture can be affirmed as true--as the Word of God. Culture must yield primacy to the Biblical revelation.

Here we must resist the temptation to set the authority of Christ over against that of Holy Writ. If Christ is Lord, then His high regard for Scripture ought to be exemplified in His disciples. They accept its instruction, trust its promises, and act upon its commands.

The way now opens before us. "We intend to resist the appeal of syncretism, which results from a low view of Scripture; we also mean to withstand what some have called *radical displacement* (the uncritical exchange of one's culture for another), which results from a low view of culture."[16] We strive instead to steer a course between these unacceptable alternatives.

It remains to see what progress we can make at the present. Edwin Gaustad argues that dissent "is not a social disease."[17] Whereupon, he adds that sometimes "the dissenter turns out to be a saint, more often he does not. Sometimes he prevails, more often he does not. Sometimes it is safe to ignore him, more often it is not."[18] He consequently cautions the dissenter against rash behavior, and others from disregarding his/her protest.

If, as Gaustad insists, dissent is not categorically wrong; it may not be wrong when expressed in defense of cultural integrity. It is proper to resist religious colonialism, whatever the source and whenever the imposition. This is not to advocate sycreticism but authenticate Christianity.

We must conversely proceed with deliberate care, lest we court the favor of man and thereby the disfavor of God. The burden for translating the gospel into any given culture lies ultimately with the national Christians, in conjunction with expatriate Christians and non-Christian nationals. The enterprise must not be carried on in isolation, for that will certainly result in dismal failure.

There is another justification for denominational dissent. It is called for when the established church becomes apostate. In this connection, Mead reminds us that dissent is often an effort to return to the faith once promulgated and henceforth binding. Dissent in this instance may be the only avenue left open to conscience.

Scripture provides a fixed point of reference for subsequent generations, in differing cultures. If we think of this as a fusion of horizons (a common metaphor), then the former remains constant while the latter changes. Scripture is without exception our authoritative rule for faith and practice.

This brings us to consider what may be called *excessive denominationalism*. It occurs when we extend our efforts beyond the legitimate concern to contextualize the gospel. It accounts for what Niebuhr criticizes as an accommodation to social caste. It also illustrates what Dawson castigates as an uncritical crusade for change.

We thereupon turn to the sage advice of Dietrich Bonhoeffer, who observes that a disciple "needs another Christian who speaks God's Word to him. He needs him again and again when he becomes uncertain and discouraged, for by himself he cannot help himself without belying the truth."[19] *The truth* involves being in Christ, and being assured that the word of one's brother is stronger than one's own. Herewith, Bonhoeffer introduces us to what it means to live in community: to be available to others, and allow others to be available to us.

Excessive denominationalism follows in the wake of our failure to recognize others in community. It is evidence that we are promoting *our* rights at the expense of our common positioning in *Christ's* body. In this connection, Hans Kung once observed that no one should disapprove papal authority so long as it did not imply privileged position and merely a greater opportunity to serve. In any case, when we consider that Christ confronts us in others, with reciprocal obligations, we are well on our way to combating the excess to which denominations may drive us.

This is not an appeal to positive thinking; it is, if anything, an appeal to *realistic thinking*. Bonhoeffer observes that Christian brotherhood is not an ideal that we must achieve, but it is rather a reality created by God in Christ in which we may participate. The more clearly we learn to recognize that the ground and strength and promise of all our fellowship is in Jesus Christ alone, the more serenely shall we think of our fellowship and pray and hope for it.[20]

The only ecumenical enterprise worthy of our support is that which draws us closer to Christ, and therein to one another. All else resembles a patchwork quilt, meant to give an impression of unity. It consequently pretends too much, and offers too little.

Bonhoeffer elsewhere asserts that through "the call of Jesus men become individuals."[21] That is, they are free to develop their own distinctiveness. They can give up on trying to carbon-copy others. Moreover, what they assume for themselves, they should happily allow for others.

We must, all things considered, be true to ourselves. We must, all things considered, encourage others to be true to themselves. This is the course of constructive diversity. It is also the way by which we actualize our unity. Denominationalism otherwise understood is not worthy of even momentary consideration.

Even so, we promote denominationalism reluctantly, lest in seeking to cure the ills of the established church, we create a worse situation. The problems we seek to escape from, more times than not, we take with us. We are called to confess our sins and seek forgiveness, followed by giving more zealous attention to our ministry. We must not allow unfavorable circumstances or promising resolutions to obscure such a noble calling.

Summary

This final exploration into the realm of denominationalism has taken a decidedly pastoral turn. We are encouraged to think of others, and how we might serve them. In return, we are likewise admonished to be open to how Christ might have them serve us. Moreover, we are individually and collectively to be open to God's creative guidance. In this manner, we may in large measure overcome the undesirable features of denominationalism, and maximize its advantages.

We sense an affinity between our conclusion and that of Mead's appeal to functional unity. Nevertheless, we cannot ignore the concern expressed by Dawson and Niebuhr concerning form. We allow that form can either contribute to or inhibit the pursuit of community. On the other hand, the former is assuredly not a substitute for the latter.

We suggest that contextualism be considered as a key to the

denominational dynamic. It provides needed insight into what is valid and invalid in the denominational appeal. It further helps us recognize the problems that give rise to dissent. It still further incorporates much of what is current to denominational theory, and offers direction for church renewal.

Editorial note. The above was an expression of growing interest in cross-cultural studies, as a natural expansion of a core concern with theological anthropology. It eventually led to the publication of three related books: *Doing Theology Across Cultures* (1982), *Making the Gospel Relevant* (1986), and *Revelation Across Cultures* (1995). In the process, I came to differentiate between the cultural and transcultural, and it was in the latter connection that I wrote the forthcoming paper in response to Helmut Thielicke's provocative treatment of myth in theological discourse.

ENDNOTES

1. Christopher Dawson, *The Dividing of Christendom*, p. 17.
2. Ibid., pp. 17-18.
3. Ibid., p. 18.
4. H. Richard Niebuhr, *The Social Sources of Denominationalism*, p. 25.
5. Ibid.
6. Ibid., p. 21.
7. Ibid., p. 26.
8. Ibid., p. 280.
9. Winthrop Hudson, *Religion in America*, p. 81.
10. Ibid.
11. Ibid., p. 82.
12. Hans Kung, *The Church*, p. 84.
13. Sidney Mead, "Denominationalism: The Shape of American Protestantism in America," *Denominationalism* (Richy, ed.), p. 75.
14. Ibid.
15. Ibid., pp. 75-105.
16. Morris Inch, *Doing Theology Across Cultures*, p. 24.
17. Edwin Gaustad, *Dissent in American Religion*, p. 2.
18. Ibid., p. 18.
19. Dietrich Bonhoeffer, *Life Together*, p. 23.
20. Ibid., p. 30.
21. Dietrich Bonhoeffer, *The Cost of Discipleship*, p. 105.

BIBLIOGRAPHY

Bonhoeffer, Dietrich. *The Cost of Discipleship.* New York: Macmillan, 1963.
_____. *Life Together.* New York: Harper & Row, 1954.
Dawson, Christopher. *The Dividing of Christendom.* Garden City: Image, 1967.
Gaustad, Edwin. *Dissent in American Religion.* Chicago: University of Chicago, 1973.
Hudson, Winthrop. *Religion in America.* New York: Scribners, 1981.
Inch, Morris. *Doing Theology Across Cultures.* Grand Rapids: Baker, 1982.
Kung, Hans. *The Church.* New York: Sheed & Ward, 1967.
Mead, Sidney. "Denominationalism: The Shape of Protestantism in America," *Denominationalism* (Richey, ed.), 70-105.
Niebuhr, H. Richard. *The Social Sources of Denominationalism.* New York: Meridian, 1957.
Richey, Russell (ed.). *Denominationalism.* Nashville: Abingdon, 1977.

MYTH IN THEOLOGICAL DISCOURSE

Should we introduce the notion of *myth* into theology, and if so, in what connection? Helmut Thielicke assumes that we should, and proceeds to clarify how and with what qualifications. We shall want to review his arresting treatment of the topic, and interact with it.

Discussion

James Packer explains that "the Greek word *mythos* means an imaginative and fictitious tale, as distinct from a narrative of observed or reconstructed events. As such, myth is neither scientific nor historical, nor factually informative in any ordinary sense."[1] Accordingly, Paul urges his readers not to "devote themselves to myths and endless genealogies rather than God's work--which is by faith" (1 Tim. 1:4), nor to heed those who "turn their ears away from the truth and turn aside to myths" (2 Tim. 4:4). So also Peter declares that "we did not follow cleverly invented stories when we told you about the power and coming of our Lord Jesus Christ, but we were eyewitnesses of his majesty" (2 Pet. 1:16).

The apostles thus contrasted myth to what they witnessed, and faith grounded on credible evidence. They repudiated myth as the speculative, imaginative alternative to the historical acts of God.

We might dismiss myth from theology on the above grounds except for the refinement that Thielicke brings to the topic. Every interpreter, according to him, must weigh how far temporal words are simply the vehicle of God's truth and to what extent they become normative for future generations. A simple aversion to myth does not alter the hermeneutic dilemma that will not go away.

Thielicke, succinctly stated, views myth as a temporal expression of eternal truth.

Thus the story of Peter's denial seems to be only about a police action and its consequences, about everyday people, ...but behind the everyday guise is a basic event. Peter exemplifies conflict and a situation of decision. An action on earth, irrespective of its concrete here-and-now reality, signifies not only itself but something else as well, which relates to eternal and not just to temporal destiny.[2]

More precisely, myth incorporates an awareness of a transcendent dimension to the situation, and the insight this throws on man's character and obligation. It focuses, in other words, on the divine-human encounter.

Myth thus understood tempts us to commit idolatry by making absolute the partial, and in doing so to take advantage of others in furthering self-interest. We use myth as a leverage to further our rebellion against God, and to justify the oppression of our fellow-persons.

Thielicke suggests that we resolve this problem not by disregarding but restraining myth. This allows us to appreciate the wonder and mystery of God, and the integrity of persons as a basis for building community. Thielicke uses the designation *kerygmatic* to describe the adulterous use of myth, and *disarmed* as its restrained alternative.

Having been alerted to the parameters of Thielicke's thinking, we can trace his rationale. The gospel stands in contrast to kerygmatic myth at two points. "First, time is no longer fleeting but unconditional. God makes *kairos*, the acceptable time (2 Cor. 6:2), the place of the mighty works of God (Acts 2:1) in which he 'lavishes himself' in time (Luther), giving my moment of life the stamp of decision."[3] We are thereby no longer enslaved *to* fate but delivered *by* faith.

"Second, time, having this goal of salvation, rushes on to its end. It moves forward from prophecy to fulfilment, from faith to sight, that God may be all in all (1 Cor. 15:28). Time is now linear, moving irreversibly to the set goal."[4] Salvation history may be said to triumph over myth.

The victory of the gospel over kerygmatic myth not only leaves the battlefield strewn with former gods but disarms myth to be creatively employed. "The statues of the gods have been broken to pieces and can be made into new mosaics."[5]

We now want to retrace our steps and take note of some related matters. I concur with Thielicke that the Word of God appears as the words of men. We consequently cannot escape asking how truth given in a particular time and situation can be construed as normative for all time and occasion. Shall we require women to cover their heads during public worship, always--sometimes--never?

Moreover, once we admit that hermeneutics involves a cultural/historical dimension, we are hard pressed to ignore myth in the sense of viewing eternal verities through temporal situations. No more than could Paul when the Lystrans confused him with Hermes (Acts 14:12), or when he alluded to the Athenian altar *To an Unknown God* (Acts 17:23). Kerygmatic myth thus confronts us on every side, waiting to be disarmed by the gospel. We nevertheless must take care not to weaken the Biblical antithesis between faith and myth. We proceed therefore with the greatest of care.

Let us first look more closely at the nature of myth, and then make such adjustments that may be called for with regard to Thielicke's reasoning. Myth may be viewed as existing in three forms: the cosmic, ethnic, and psychic. Cosmic myth pertains to our common experience on planet earth. It derives from observing the sun rise, creep across the sky, and hide behind the horizon--only to appear in a similar fashion not many hours removed. It also ties into our corporate experience of that phenomenon: how we discuss the matter, celebrate it, tell stories concerning it, and set our watches by it. Cosmic myth likewise encourages us to speculate on the ultimate meaning of life: what purpose may bring us and it (the natural creation) into existence, sustains it all in order, and provokes our minds to question.

Other myths draw from the distinctive experience of some segment of humanity, at least initially so. Thereafter, they may be disseminated more broadly, prompted and enriched in return. These are more lineal than the cosmic myths, which tend toward a cyclical perspective--following the order of day and night, the season, whatever seems repeatable in our common experience. The ethnic myths relate to the experience of a particular group of persons as they reflect on the past, spinning their accounts at day's end, to magnify their accomplishments and admonish their youth.

Psychic myth is more or less peculiar to a given individual. It involves one's self-image, and is the source from which we draw autobiography and testimony. It resists the incursion of others, except by invitation and then only for a hasty look around.

These myths (cosmic, ethnic, and psychic) wrestle with reality and jostle one another for position. They never pin down the reality they witness to, but are human convention intended to identify, reflect upon, and communicate reality insofar as we understand it.

Myths also compete with one another, as illustrated by the pestiferous Greek pantheon. One seems to gain the ascendance for the moment, until outwitted by another or overcome by brute force.

Having differentiated among the forms of myth, we can speak more pointedly concerning our approach to them--whether as an individual or corporately. We should not make absolute some feature of cosmic myth, as with Romanticism; ethnic myth, as has Marxism; or psychic myth, as would Existentialism. We ought not to take our respective myths that seriously.

Even so, myth of whatever variety reminds us of our distinctive human character. In one connection, we recall our common bond; in another, our peculiar legacy; in still another, one's personal identity. In all these connections, the psalmist reflects: "What is man that you are mindful of him, the son of man that you care for him? You made him a little lower than the heavenly beings and crowned him with glory and honor" (8:4-5).

Thielicke calls our attention to the incarnation as free from myth. He reasons as follows: "The incarnation...does not really point away from itself to something else, as myth does. Quite nonmythically and nonsymbolically it points to itself."[6] It draws our attention not away from but to history, as the focus of God's redemptive activity.

Not only that, but the incarnation occurred within the course of salvation history. "In the past God spoke to our forefathers through the prophets at many times and in various ways, but in these last days he has spoken to us by his Son, whom he appointed heir of all things, and through whom he made the universe" (Heb. 1:1-2). God provided a cultural-historical womb to receive Jesus' birth, life, and teaching. He called out a select people from all the others, labored to instill in them the necessary ideals, and when the time was ripe brought forth the Christ.

Moreover, myth must bow to the announcement that Jesus is Lord. He transcends our cherished imaginations as the Other that meets us here in our current situation. Myth retreats as faith takes over.

Freedom follows on the heels of faith. "So if the Son sets you free, you will be free indeed" (John 8:36). Free from pretense; free to reality. This occurs when formal religion gives way to a vital relationship.

Thielicke draws the implication for this newly found freedom for creative expression. (We will enlarge on his observation before touching on additional considerations.) "Only in virtue of this (mythic quality) can the everyday enjoy literary status."[7] Only by way of myth can we feel the pulse of life. Only as we disarm myth can we relate to the reality of God's world: His presence and that of others.

We should not confuse *perspective* with *performance*, as the following combinations would suggest:

1. good perspective, good performance
2. good perspective, bad performance
3. bad perspective, bad performance
4. bad perspective, good performance

We have listed the alternatives in order of preference, from one through four. The preference for bad over good performance may not at first appear evident. It is that whereas bad performance may alert us to a bad perspective, good performance conceals the larger difficulty.

Kerygmatic myth inclines to settle for convention. It hesitates to turn a new phrase, attempt an alternative construction, or experiment with a wider vocabulary. It slavishly employs language as if the gods had decreed the manner in which it should be observed.

Disarmed myth recognizes language as a God-ordained means to achieve a God-approved purpose. It reasons that since we are made in God's image, we were meant to be creative. As a result, it scatters the gods to allow for a rich diversity of praise to our Maker.

Herewith, we introduce the notion of *festivity*, to be distinguished from *frivolity*. "Frivolity is the painted smile on a terminally sick patient. Its waggishness springs not from a joyous confidence in the ultimate goodness of life but from a despairing failure to make any sense out of it."[8] Festivity affirms life as God's gift, frivolity throws up its hands in resignation; festivity takes pleasure in what life has to offer; frivolity anesthetizes the human spirit.

Two ways beckon to us, and we must decide between them. The one is that of grateful acceptance, and the other of thankless persistence (cf. Rom. 1:21). If we plod ahead, life degenerates around us; but if we take to higher ground, life becomes increasingly rewarding. Festivity consequently lies at the crossroads of life, and disarmed myth urges us to assume our noble calling.

Disarmed myth likewise provides access to social change. It allows us to conceive what is not but could be. It as a result turns our persisting obstacles into inviting opportunities.

On the other hand, disarmed myth creates dissatisfaction with the *status quo*. This reminds us that our most subtle enemy is not evil, but the good that substitutes for the better. There is always new ground to be gained.

This constructive approach to life must be distinguished from mere novelty. We ought not to advocate change for the sake of change, but so as to achieve some worthwhile end. Not because it is politically correct, but because it offers a genuine potential.

Disarmed myth moreover guides us in the expression of our catholic (universal) faith. Positively, it allows us to express our faith in ways that are culturally meaningful. Negatively, it reminds us that these are not the only ways in which eternal verities can be expressed.

By way of example, we feel inhibited in singing God's praise in a foreign tongue. We worship more readily when we can use our own language and idiom. Even so, we can appreciate sharing with those of other cultural orientation. Disarmed myth frees us to enjoy mutual enrichment, especially when it involves those with cultural backgrounds diverse from our own.

Summary

Now, to sum up:

1. Helmut Thielicke suggests that we need to consider myth as critical to our hermeneutic task. Inasmuch as hermeneutics involves a cultural/historical exploration, and myth serves as a commonly accepted term for describing man's perception of eternal truths, his point appears well taken.

2. Even so, we should not proceed without giving due consideration to the Biblical contrast between faith founded on credible evidence and ingenious fables. Myth in the narrow sense of *an imaginative and fictitious tale*, as distinct from *a narrative of observed or reconstructed events* must be categorically rejected.

3. This allows us to consider Thielicke's distinction between *kerygmatic* and *disarmed myth*. The former infests creation with gods meant to satisfy our personal predilection, and justify our perverse behavior. The latter repudiates idolatry, so as to enable us to honor God, and minister to one another.

4. The gospel disarms kerygmatic myth via the incarnation. First, in that the incarnation bridges the myth barrier. Second, in that it transforms myth in the process. All this is cast in the context of salvation history.

5. We may refine myth into cosmic, ethnic, and psychic categories. These, in turn, refer to common experience, that of some particular group, and as unique to individuals. This refinement helps us appreciate what subtle forms idolatry can take, and how vigorously we must press Jesus' lordship over life in all its aspects.

6. Disarmed myth serves those who embrace Jesus as Lord. While Thielicke illustrates this in connection with literary creativity, we have added festivity, social progress, and the confession of our catholic faith

as prime examples. Other cases in point could be readily added, but these are quite sufficient to suggest that life becomes creatively open when Christ disarms kerygmatic myth. Myth thereupon no longer rules as tyrant but serves as minister.

Editorial note. This article is best considered in juxtaposition to *Understanding Bible Prophecy* (1977), which helps to clarify my conception of *salvation history.* Soon after reading this paper I took a hiatus from writing in order to focus my attention on overseas responsibilities. It was not until the latter ran its course that I again *took pen in hand*, accounting for the remaining papers.

ENDNOTES

1. James Packer, "Myth," *Baker's Dictionary of Christian Ethics* (Henry, ed.),
   p. 441.
2. Helmut Thielicke, *The Evangelical Faith*, p. 73.
3. Ibid., pp. 85-86.
4. Ibid., p. 86.
5. Ibid., p. 100.
6. Ibid., pp. 82-83.
7. Ibid., p. 73.
8. Harvey Cox, *The Feast of Fools*, p. 26.

BIBLIOGRAPHY

Cox, Henry. *The Feast of Fools*. New York: Harper & Row, 1969.

Henry, Carl H. (ed.). *Baker's Dictionary of Christian Ethics*. Grand Rapids: Baker, 1973.

Packer, James. "Myth," *Baker's Dictionary of Christian Ethics* (Henry, ed.), 441- 442.

Thielicke, Helmut. *The Evangelical Faith*. Grand Rapids: Eerdmans, 1974.

UP TO THE PRESENT

Our time abroad allowed more occasion for thought than organizing it to share with others. Upon our return, all this changed. Once again I could pursue the sometimes illusive trail of theological anthropology.

Only one of the papers included in this section has as it were *seen the light of day. Shalom in Black and White* was read at an annual Wheaton College Theological Conference, dealing with race relations. This allowed me to reflect on the significance of racial reconciliation in theological perspective. *Salvation Formulae in Luke-Acts* and *Fuzzy Set Theology* work from different ends of a continuum: the former with regard to the critical juncture where faith takes over to transform life, and the latter to balance a prevailing concern for theological precision. *Chaos as the Crucible of Faith* and *Chaos and the Moral Imperative* enlarge on a continuing interest in chaos theory, evidenced earlier with the publication of *Chaos Paradigm: A Theological Exploration* (1998). All things considered, we push back the horizons of our understanding concerning the perennial question: "What is man?"

SHALOM IN BLACK AND WHITE

I should like to take this opportunity to briefly trace my modest contribution to the general topic of this conference (concerning race reconciliations). This will pave the way for discussing *shalom* (peace, well-being) in black and white. Initially, a narrative format will add an existential insight otherwise lacking.

Reflecting Back

My youth was spent in rural Maine. There were no black folk living in own town nor were there many nearby. My first recollection concerns a circus roustabout, whose dark skin glistened on a hot summer day.

A black unit was assigned to guard a railway bridge a few miles from our village during World War II. Our high school baseball team played their squad, and were soundly beaten. I had the unfortunate experience of pitching that game, and remember feeling thoroughly frustrated and not a little embarrassed.

Martin Luther King and I were awarded our doctorates from Boston University the same year. In those days, no one pointed him out for subsequent honors. I was serving a parish in South Boston, and our paths seldom crossed.

"When two young Olympians raised their black gloved hands from the victors' podium in Mexico City last fall, they may have symbolized more than they or we recognized."[1] So I introduced an article for *Christianity Today*. The year was 1969. It was an effort to put black power into perspective. I took that occasion to warn against equating the Kingdom of God with any human enterprise, whether with the white establishment or black protest. God invites both black and white into His future, imperfectly realized at the present.

Black theology is one of the few theological innovations credited to

American ingenuity. It is still a relatively new phenomenon, in its formative stage, and much in ferment. Given the uncertainty surrounding the nature of black theology, James Cone is perhaps its most exacting spokesman.[2]

It was a decade later. I chose to focus my attention on Cone's Christological methodology.

It seemed to me that Cone was working his Christology related to *what* Christ was doing in the world today, especially concerning the oppressed. I agreed with Bonhoeffer that the prior question concerned *who*, i.e., the issue of transcendence rather than immanence. This being the case, "Wolfhart Pannenberg in the title of his work on Christology anticipates the direction in which one must develop an orthodox Christological confession: *Jesus, God, and Man.*"[3]

The conciliatory character with which I closed the article sets the tone for the discussion to follow:

> Cone has done us a significant service in probing the perspective of black consciousness. My own remarks are offered in the spirit of theological dialogue. Through candid dialogue we may come to better understand and more faithfully apply the truth once revealed.[4]

I published in 1986 two articles on traditional African religions.[5] My capable informants were Nigerian students Danjum Dingba and Bluff Obiomah. They reflected respectively on the Nkada view of sin, and the Uview perspective on sacrifice.

It was primarily during two short term assignments in West Africa that I experienced what Billy Graham alludes to as becoming *a world Christian*. One situation especially stands out in my memory. I was asked to participate in an ordination service. When invited to join with others in laying hands on the young man's head, I looked down amazed to see one large white hand virtually lost in a sea of smaller black hands. I felt overwhelmed by the awesome inclusive character thus evidenced in Christian fellowship.

My African sojourn accented the rich cultural diversity of the native people. There were reported to be over 250 tribal languages represented in Nigeria alone.

It also made me wonder what African legacy might be carried over into the Afro-American experience. I could at least agree with Pierre van den Berghe that the "romantic search for survivals of African culture is elusive."[6] This was driven home to me when an Afro-American arrived to assist in our ministry. My African students had been looking forward with great anticipation to this event, but were disappointed to find that his cultural perspective was more similar to us *orange skins* (so designated because we resembled the inside of an orange) than their own.

"We have seen how limited the melting pot metaphor proves to be in the light of selected sub-cultures."[7] So I concluded in a hermeneutical article, exploring Native American and Afro-American receiving cultures. Even so, I pointed out that these might best be understood over against a WASP cultural norm (which has led some to label Afro-Americans as *Afro-Saxons*). However understood, they represent unique receptor audiences for Biblical revelation. The past is prologue. I continue to reflect on the above concerns in context of what is locally referred to as *The New South*. More particularly, from our retirement home in Arkansas.

Pressing On

Ethnicity is no illusion.

> Our species has developed an impressive bag of tricks, called culture, to control, modify, indeed create an important part of our environment. Culture is part of our environment, but it differs from the rest of it in being created and transmitted by our species according to mechanisms fundamentally different from genetic natural selection.[8]

Ethnicity by implication derives essentially from common descent.

Sometimes ethnic identity must be established quickly. When that is the case, we rely on appearance, dress, or behavior. We employ the term *race* to single out a people group by inherited phenotypical characteristics (appearance).

America qualifies by consensus as multi-ethnic and multi-racial. In some ways, it is becoming more so, and in some ways less.

There is much at stake concerning how we view our pluralistic heritage. If, for instance, we think that for all practical purposes in terms of a cultural melting pot, this could take the edge off affirmative action.

Of course, the melting pot metaphor is only one of several ways promoted to characterize American ethnicity. Gerald Postiglione lists five alternatives: Anglo-conformity, melting pot, cultural pluralism, emerging culture, and impact-integration.[9] We will review these briefly in order.

The *Anglo-conformity* option originated in the seventeenth century, when English settlers dominated others and succeeded in establishing their ways as culturally normative. It was firmed up and popularized in the late nineteenth and early twentieth centuries.[10]

The graphic *melting pot* alternative was introduced to account for the various ingredients involved in the great Atlantic migration. While dating to the eighteenth century, it was not popularized until the early twentieth century.[11]

The *cultural pluralism* perspective meant to account for the resistance of ethnic groups to assimilation. It was refined during the twentieth century to allow for ethnic interaction and the embracing of common traits.[12]

The *emerging culture* model is of more recent vintage, dating to the 1970s.[13] It pointed out that where each ethnic group was different from one another, it also differed from its original heritage. This legitimizes our speaking of Afro- and Anglo-Americans as distinct from the cultures of their respective origins.

Close on the heels of the preceding, the *impact-integration* thesis suggests that ethnic groups collide in such a way as to fuse (or integrate).[14] Reflecting this opinion, James Baldwin observes "my own experience proves to me that the connection between American whites and blacks is far deeper and more passionate than many of us like to think."[15]

This plethora of models reveal how complex a cultural phenomenon we experience. Its more obvious components would appear to be (1) ethnic plurality, (2) tendency toward reciprocal accommodation, (3) Anglo-prominence in the cultural mix, (4) as modified by successive waves of minority immigration, (5) as resisted by certain groups more than others--sometimes of necessity and other times voluntarily, (6) not uncommonly in romanticized form, (7) resulting in new ethnicities distinct not only from one another but their cultural antecedents, (8) impacting so as to fuse together, (9) as a result, bonded together for better and worse, and (10) sometimes expressing confidence and other times uncertainty.

These set the parameters within which we experience or fail to experience *shalom*, except as they may be transformed by some inherent or imposed means. This is, in sociological perspective, *our* reality.

On the other hand, God is the ultimate source of *shalom*. He shares *His* peace with others in accordance to such conditions as are appropriate. In this connection see Galatians 6:16, Ephesians 6:25, 1 Peter 5:14, and 3 John 14.

Shalom is moreover an illusive commodity because of its seemingly endless connotations. Qualifications aside, it "is an announcement that God has a vision of how the world shall be and is not yet. And the faith affirmed in the church is the twin resolve that was meant to discern God's vision of what the world shall be and that we mean to live toward that vision."[16]

Shalom as freedom. Scripture makes it eminently clear that God would free us from the bondage of sin, and free us to serve His holy resolve. "Let my people go," Moses spoke at God's bequest, "so that they may hold a festival to me in the desert" (Exod. 5:1). "So if the Son sets you free," Jesus assured those standing by, "you shall be free indeed" (John 8:36).

With such in mind, we listen in on Paul's curious interchange with Agrippa. The latter protested the apostle's zealous appeal: "Do you think that in such a short time you can persuade me to be a Christian? (Acts 26:28). Perhaps embarrassed before his Roman associates, he intended to ridicule Paul's sincere effort.

"Short time or long," the apostle held his ground, "I pray God that not only you but all who are listening to me today may become what I am, except for these chains." This would seem to suggest that while spiritual and physical freedom are not synonymous, they similarly reflect the *shalom* ideal. (Note especially the exception clause in this connection.)

If this thesis should hold, the Biblical *allowance* for slavery might be thought analogous to divorce. Concerning the latter, Jesus observed: "Moses permitted you to divorce your wives because your hearts were hard. But it was not this way from the beginning" (Matt. 19:8). *In the beginning,* according to the Genesis narrative, man was born free.

As for American slavery, we need to sift fact from fiction. It would appear that Africans were targeted primarily because of their availability, although the action was sometimes justified on the basis of race. In any case, there was more than enough blame to spread around. Involved in the slave trade were native chiefs, Arab traders, and European merchant marine.

The plantation economy thrived to the south and east of our present location, where land could be cleared and crops planted. The plantation owner generally viewed himself as a benevolent despot, both as relates to his family and slave populations. For instance, the relationship between the Bullocks and their slaves "had many aspects of an extended family. No matter what they thought of one another and no matter what the legal arrangements were, these people, regardless of color, were bound together not only by the present necessity, but also by common past."[17]

Margaret Bolsterli further concludes that if Arkansas were compared with the Garden of Eden, slavery would be its serpent. According to

Bolsterli, serpentine slavery would undermine plantation society, and "cast a curse on its perpetrators for generations to come."

"In 1860, on the eve of the emancipation, there were about 350,000 slave owners in the United States--1.3% of the country's whites. Among them, they owned some 3,952,000 slaves, for an average of only a little over 11 slaves per owner,"[18] The median would have been still less, since large plantations would increase the average.

Contrary to popular thought, slave families were not as a rule separated. On the contrary, it better served the owners to have stable slave families, for morale and to discourage escape. Such practical considerations were not uncommonly accompanied by humanitarian and/or religious concerns.

While the wanton death of a single person is intolerable, the "number of Chinese killed within a few days, at various times in the history of southeast Asia, has on a number of occasions exceeded all the blacks ever lynched in the history of the United States."[19] So writes a black author, citing studies done with regard to violence perpetuated against minorities.

Even so, none appear immune from abusing those under their control, given the opportunity to do so without impunity. Another black writer observes: "If one is permitted to treat any group of people with special disfavor because of their skin, there is no limit to what one will force them to endure, and, since the entire race has been mysteriously indicted, no reason not to attempt to destroy it root and branch."[20]

All things considered, it would seem safe to conclude that slavery runs counter to the *shalom* ideal. Where for a time tolerated, it was because of our *hardness of heart.* In the beginning, it was not so; in the end, it will not be.

Shalom as unity. Ignatius unequivocally affirmed that "there is one nature, and one family of mankind."[21] In support of his claim, he reminds us that in Christ gender, cultural, racial, and social barriers are set aside (cf. Gal. 3:28). The church experiences what, ideally speaking, God would have of others by embracing *shalom* unity.

Jessie Jackson's familiar refrain *but I am somebody* seems *apropos.* I may be black, but I am somebody. I may be white, but I am somebody. Since I am human, I am somebody.

This suggests to me being there for others, allowing them to be there for me, and openness toward God. Reality unfortunately falls considerably short of the ideal.

As for reality from black perspective, "integration has always worked very well in the South, after the sun goes down." "And in exactly the same way that the South imagines that it *knows* the Negro, the North imagines that it has set him free. Both camps are deluded." "Neither the Southerner nor the Northerner is able to look on the Negro simply as a man. It seems to be indispensable to the national self-esteem that the Negro be considered either as a kind of ward or as a victim."[22]

"The civil rights vision," according to Thomas Sowell, "tends to dichotomize the spectrum of possible reasons for group difference into (1) discrimination and (2) innate inferiority. Rejecting the latter, they are left with the former."[23] *Ipso facto* blacks regardless of circumstances are victims.

Conversely, Sowell insists that complex sociological factors are at work. "Blacks are a decade younger than the Japanese. Jews are a quarter of a century older than Puerto Ricans. Polish Americans are twice as old as American Indians." "Even if the various racial and ethnic groups were identical in every other respect, their age difference alone would prevent their being equally represented kin occupations requiring experience or higher education."[24]

Cultural mores further differentiate ethnic groups. Half of Mexican American wives were married in their teens, while only 10% of Japanese American wives. As for blacks, they may all look alike to a racist, but various segments of the black community strikingly differ from one another. For instance, those of West Indian origin (such as Colin Powell) enter the professional ranks at about twice the rate of blacks in general, and slightly higher than the American population as a whole.

It seems to Sowell a short step from *victim* to *ward*. We inadvertently make the transition when shifting our efforts from achieving equal opportunities to insuring comparable results.

Affirmative action would seem to have better served the interests of advantaged blacks and their paternalistic white benefactors than the black community as a whole. In defense of this conclusion, Sowell points out the substantial gains made prior to affirmative action, and mixed results thereafter. Finally, he calls our attention to opinion polls suggesting that most blacks oppose preferential treatment.[25]

In conclusion, we must affirm our common human identity in keeping with the *shalom* ideal. In the words of the legendary basketball player Julius Erving (alias Dr. J.): "I believe in one race, the human race." We consequently must resist the temptation to regard persons simply as *victims*, on their way to becoming *wards*, and in the process robbing them of human dignity.

Shalom as justice. I served for some time with the black social activist

John Perkins on the Social Action Committee of the National Association of Evangelicals. He would whenever I offered a prayer for *shalom* follow it up with a prayer for *justice*, as if to remind us that we could not enjoy the former without the latter.

"One of the running debates in contemporary theology has to do with the relation of social justice to the higher righteousness of the kingdom of God," Donald Bloesch observes.

> The first advocates freedom and equality in the economic and political areas of life; the second heralds the liberty of the children of God. In a society ruled by the norms of justice, we treat one another as equals. But in the kingdom of God we embrace one another as brothers and sisters in Christ.[26]

Social justice serves as a sign of or witness to this higher righteousness. It also resembles a stepping-stone, in that it creates "a thirst in people for the holiness and goodness of God."

From still another perspective, social justice appears as a fruit or consequence of kingdom righteousness. It reflects human cooperation with God's purposes. It operates much as would a dutiful son in making his father's wishes his own.

If one person is denied justice, it is as if all have been denied. When justice triumphs in one connection, all benefit. What God would bestow on one, He would extend to all.

In a passage Perkins delighted in quoting, "But let justice roll on like a river, righteousness like a never-failing stream!" (Amos 5:24). The similes remind us of the seasonal rains, when the tributaries could hardly contain the rush of water. Whereupon, the river surges on its way to refresh the parched earth, which in turn brings forth abundant produce. In like manner, justice/righteousness can be said to revive society.

Shalom as variously experienced. Walter Brueggemann suggests that *shalom* appears differently from the perspectives of the socially advantaged and deprived. That is, from the *haves* and *have-nots*.

This is a provocative insight, which Brueggemann takes up in reverse order. "First, let me report on the Moses-Joshua-Samuel prophetic tradition. This is the one we know best and the one most of us consider as *normative* for the Bible."[27] Liberation theologians, as an example, focus on this alternative.

Biblical illustrations abound, as when oppressed "you cried to me for help, did I not save you from their hands?" (Judg. 10:12). Or again, "do not stop crying out to the Lord our God for us, that he may rescue us from the hand of the Philistines" (1 Sam. 7:8).

Shalom from the point of view of one socially deprived involves deliverance from oppression, provision for life's necessities, and a sense of personal integrity. God consequently enjoined the Hebrews not to oppress the alien because "you yourselves know how it feels to be aliens" (Exod. 22:9). Foster instead a society void of oppressors and oppressed.

Cultivate also a society where those impoverished are cared for. "Do not go over the vineyard a second time or pick up the grapes that have fallen. Leave them for the poor and the alien. I am the Lord your God" (Lev. 19:10). *I am your God* may suggest that God will hold them accountable, that He will reward their generosity, or most likely, both. In any case, both emphases can readily be documented from the prophetic literature.

Create finally a society were people respect others and respect themselves. "A good name is more desirable," the sage confesses, "than great riches; to be esteemed is better than silver or gold" (Prov. 22:1).

Excerpts selected from the statement of intent of the 1980 Consultation of the Theology of Development will serve to illustrate *shalom* as advocated for the socially deprived:

> We are deeply disturbed by the human suffering present in the agonizing realities of hunger, malnutrition, disease, unemployment, illiteracy, deprivation and starvation.

> We are deeply disturbed that the difference in standards of living between the rich and poor continues to increase.

> We resolve to encourage, by all peaceful and constructive means available to us, the poor and oppressed who are seeking to establish a position of dignity and self-worth.[28]

Brueggemann turns our attention from those deprived to privileged persons. As for the Biblical narrative, we shift triads from Moses, Joshua, and Samuel to Noah, Abraham, and David.

Examples also abound in this connection. For instance, God promised the patriarch Noah: "As long as the earth endures, seedtime and harvest, cold and heat, summer and winter, day and night will never cease" (Gen. 8:22). So also He pledges to David concerning his successor: "But my love will never be taken away from him... . Your house and your kingdom will endure forever before me: your throne will be established forever" (2 Sam. 7:15-16).

Shalom thus conceived expresses appreciation for God's rich provision, and constant faithfulness. We are reminded how God paused in His creative activity to describe the results as *good*, and when He was finished, He appraised them as *very good* (Gen. 1:31). "Wherefore a man should treasure it (life), not despise it," according to Jewish tradition, "affirm and not deny it; have faith in it and never despair of its possibilities. For behind it is God."[29] Qualifications aside, life is good, and meant to be embraced with gratitude. For in cherishing the gift, we honor the Giver.

We bear witness to our appreciation by faithfully exercising our stewardship responsibilities (cf. Gen. 1:28). The good earth responds with its produce, society bonds together, and our hearts rejoice. *Shalom* reigns without, among, and within.

Use it or lose it. It is as we exercise our stewardship potential that we come to realize the purposes for which God intended us. Failing to do so, we become what T.S. Eliot refers to as *hollow men*, heads stuffed with straw, our dried voices whispering meaningless phrases.

Shalom as community. The faith community is, in a manner of speaking, a community before its time. It strides into the future not by sight but faith. Realizing that the present age is passing away, it reaches out to lay hold on that which will endure the ravages of time.

Shalom characterizes the new age. "They will neither harm nor destroy in all my holy mountain, for the earth will be full of the knowledge of the Lord as the waters cover the sea" (Isa. 11:9). "All your sons will be taught by the Lord, and great will be your children's peace" (Isa. 54:13).

Even now, Jesus' disciples would experience the earnest of the new age *shalom*. "Peace I leave with you; my peace I give you. I do not give it as the world gives (promising what it cannot provide). Let not your heart be troubled and do not be afraid" (John 14:27).

The world drags its feet. It

> wants shalom; but we know the world cannot have shalom, cannot possibly have it, on the present terms. The emergence of shalom-- wholeness for church, people, earth--requires a change in values, presuppositions and perceptions. Shalom happens only for communities engaged in empowering vulnerability.[30]

We can appreciate the world's dilemma. "Nothing is more desirable than to be released from an affliction, but nothing is more frightening than to be divested of a crutch."[31] Whereas Jesus offers healing, the world opts instead for security.

As a result, the world turns in on itself. "We become like shavings planed from a piece of wood that naturally curl around themselves. We become separated from the source of life. Our thinking, our perceptions, our ways of knowing all become distorted."[32]

God expects something better from the faith community. He anticipates that it will break loose from the *status quo*, and take leave from the city of destruction. He encourages it to press on toward the eternal city.

We cannot expect the world to sit idly by. It resents the faith community professing that which it does not share in. It feels threatened as if invaded by alien powers. It rationalizes, incriminates, and periodically persecutes Jesus' disciples.

What may at first appear as if a minor parting of the ways results, as C.S. Lewis describes it, in *the great divorce*. These two ways are not color coded. *Black and white together*, they merge either to the left or right.

One day I overheard two African elders discussing an expatriate. One observed that he was *Tommy Titcombish*, which sounded as if afflicted with some exotic disease. It was instead a reference to a pioneer West African missionary, associated in their thinking with reconciling warring people. Such should characterize the followers of Christ, as exemplars of *shalom*.

Editorial note. As affirmed above, *the past is prologue.* This maxim alerts us that we draw from the past to explore human experience in context of the *shalom* ideal. As such, it resembles *Revelation Across Cultures* (1995), *Charting a Good Church Trip* (1995), and *A Case For Christianity* (1997). The last of these, as a point of information, was in preparation well before its publication date might suggest. The next entry signals the dawn of a new day with a fresh look at the Biblical text. It has this in common with two studies: *Exhortations of Jesus According to Matthew* and *Up From the Depths: Mark as Tragedy*-- published jointly (1997).

ENDNOTES

1. Morris Inch, "Anatomy of a Symbol," p. 5.
2. Morris Inch, "Black Christology in Historical Perspective,"*Perspectives on Evangelical Theology* (Kantzer and Gundry, ed.), p. 161.
3. Ibid., p. 158.
4. Ibid., p. 162.
5. Morris Inch, *Making the Good News Relevant*, pp. 67-87.
6. Pierre van den Berghe, *The Ethnic Perspective*, p. 177.
7. Morris Inch, *Revelation Across Cultures*, p. 118.
8. Van der Berghe, *op. cit.*, p. 6.
9. Gerald Postiglione, *Ethnicty and American Social Theory*, pp. 14-23.
10. Madison Grant was an avid supporter of the Anglo-conformity premise as evidenced in *The Passing of the Great Race*. New York: Scribners, 1916. Another prime example was Henry Fairchild, *The Melting Pot Mistake*. Boston: Little, Brown, and Co., 1926.
11. The melting pot analogy was coined in a play written by Israel Langwell (*The Melting Pot*. New York: Macmillan, 1929). Will Herberg and others expanded the idea to multiple melting pots for major religious denominations. Herberg's classic text was *Catholic-Protestant-Jew*. New York: Doubleday, 1955.
12. Horace Kallen was likely its most prominent advocate in *Culture and Democracy in the United States*. New York: Doubleday, 1955. See also Louis Adamic, *My America*. New York: Harper & Row, 1938.
13. Many authors contributed in various ways to the concept of emerging cultures. One such work was Nathan Glazer and Daniel Moynihan, *Beyond the Melting Pot*. Cambridge: Massachusetts Institute of Technology, 1970. Another example was Andrew Greeley, *Ethnicity in the United States*. New York: John Willey, 1974.
14. F.X. Femminella was perhaps its most articulate spokesperson. As prime cases in point, note "The impact of Italian Migration and American Catholicism," *American Catholic Sociological Review*. Vol. 22, No. 3 (Fall, 1961), 233-241, and "Social Ramifications of Ethnicity in the Suburbs," *Ethnicity and Suburbia: The Long Island Experience* (S. LaGumina, ed.), Garden City: Nassau College, 1980.
15. James Baldwin, *Nobody Knows My Name*, p. xiii.

16. Walter Brueggemann, *Living Toward Vision*, p. 39.
17. Margaret Jones Bolsterli, *A Remembrance of Eden*, p. 4.
18. Van den Berghe, *op. cit., p. 127.*
19. Thomas Sowell, *Civil Rights: Rhetoric or Reality?* p. 22. (cf. Victor Purcell, *The Chinese in Southern Asia.* New York: Oxford University, 1980, pp. 406, 514, 519, 527).
20. James Baldwin, *The Fire Next Time*, pp. 82-83.
21. Ignatius, *To the Philadelphians.* III. 10.
22. Baldwin, *Nobody Knows My Name*, pp. 70-71, 115-116.
23. Sowell, *op. cit.*, p. 21.
24. Ibid., pp. 42-43.
25. *Gallup Opinion Index*, Report 143 (June, 1977), p. 23.
26. Donald Bloesch, *Freedom For Obedience*, pp. 83-84.
27. Brueggemann, *op. cit.*, p. 28.
28. Ronald Sider (ed.), *Evangelicals and Development*, pp. 15-16.
29. Milton Steinberg, *Basic Judaism*, p. 59.
30. Brueggemann, *op. cit.*, p. 28.
31. Baldwin, *Nobody Knows My Name*, p. xii.
32. Klyne Snodgrass, *Between Two Worlds*, p. 46.

BIBLIOGRAPHY

Baldwin, James. *The Fire Next Time*. New York: Vintage, 1993.

_____. *Nobody Knows My Name*. New York: Vintage, 1993.

Bloesch, Donald. *Freedom For Obedience*. San Francisco: Harper & Row, 1987.

Bolsterlie, Margaret Jones. *A Remembrance of Eden*. Fayetteville: University of Arkansas, 1993.

Brueggemann, Walter. *Living Toward Vision*. Philadelphia: United Church, 1976.

Gallup Opinion Index, Report 143 (June, 1977).

Ignatius. *To the Philadelphians*.

Inch Morris. "Anatomy of a Symbol," *Christianity Today*, XIII (April, 1969), 5-7.

_____. "Black Christology in Historical Perspective," *Perspectives on Evangelical Theology* (Kantzer and Gundry, eds.), 151-162.

_____. *Making the Good News Relevant*. Nashville: Thomas Nelson, 1986.

_____. *Revelation Across Cultures*. Russellville: Posey, 1995.

Kantzer, Kenneth and Stanley Gundrey (eds.). *Perspectives on Evangelical Theology*. Grand Rapids: Baker, 1979.

Postiglione, Gerald. *Ethnicity and American Social Theory*. New York: University Press of America, 1983.

Sider, Ronald (ed.). *Evangelicals and Development*. Philadelphia: Westminster, 1981.

Snodgrass, Klyne. *Between Two Worlds*. Grand Rapids: Zondervan, 1990.

Sowell, Thomas. *Civil Rights: Rhetoric or Reality?* New York: Morrow, 1984.

Steinberg, Milton. *Basic Judaism*. New York: Harcourt, Brace & World, 1947.

Van der Berge, Pierre. *The Ethnic Perspective*. New York: Elsevier, 1981.

SALVATION FORMULAE IN LUKE-ACTS

Some theological issues appear more crucial than others. I could never get excited over whether the believers after death remain alert or slumber. In either case, they are only one conscious moment away from experiencing the Lord's presence.

Salvation is quite another matter. The stakes increase dramatically. We ought therefore to approach the current topic with the utmost care, in that it determines how we shall understand our posturing in God's world.

Prolegomena

In an earlier connection, I observed:

> Luke's basic theme (in Luke-Acts) is the atoning sacrifice of Christ. Jesus is come that men everywhere may experience God's redemption. ...The sacrifice took place, not in the privileged sanctuary of a temple, but on a hill outside the city wall, where a mixed multitude wandered aimlessly to and fro.[1]

Since Luke focuses on salvation, his two volume work presents us with a likely prospect for mining the topic. The theme is usually near the surface so to invite our attention.

Even so, Luke-Acts employs a rich variety of salvation formulae. A rough count reveals thirty-six variations, either distinctive or in some combination. Illustrative of the former, belief that justifies (Acts 13:39). Illustrative of the latter, repentance used in conjunction with baptism (Acts 2:38), conversion (Acts 3:19), and the forgiveness of sins (Acts 5:31).

These may result from looking at salvation from varying perspectives, relevance to the narrative setting, effort to economize, or (as Luke reports what others said) personal preference. The factors appear individually and in combination.

Luke recalls a previous time from the perspective of his own. This results in what some have described as an overlay process, and others as a fusion of horizons. As relates to our present topic, the author would seem to view these variations as a rich salvation mosaic. He sees them as an expression of God's compassionate and creative design.

Stated differently, Luke senses no problem in reconciling such differences as may occur. He views the salvation formulae as complementary rather than competitive. Extending his rationale, we may explain the more obscure by the more obvious. Scripture is its own best interpreter.

As we have come to understand the distinction, Luke qualifies more as a Biblical than systematic theologian. The former reflects on God's revelation as it occurs in history; the latter as it can be subsequently organized. While there is order to the former, it more resembles that found in nature than in a nursery.

This suggest four things to bear in mind. First, history and therefore revelation is progressive in character. One thing follows another. Each builds upon what went before and prepares for that which will follow.

Second, revelation is incomprehensible apart from history. It is event-oriented. It is God's answer to why things happen as they do.

Third, there is continuity throughout. God does not alter truth from one day to the next. What He tells us on one occasion, He characteristically reaffirms elsewhere--sometimes with a qualification or additional information.

Finally, there is a practical intent. God does not mean simply to satisfy our curiosity but prepare us to live in His world, according to His word, and by His grace. As sometimes put, He wants us to get out of the stands and onto the playing field.

In the process of my study, I identified fifty-six passages containing salvation formulae. I selected from these ten to consider in this paper. They were chosen either because of their representative character and/or some distinctive feature. I will comment briefly on each in turn, before attempting some general conclusions.

Selected Texts

(1) John the Baptist was sent to prepare the way of the Lord, "to give his people the knowledge of salvation through the forgiveness of their sins" (Luke 1:77). His was a ministry related to salvation appropriated

through forgiveness.

Salvation suggests deliverance. Its Hebrew antecedent (*yeshuah*) implies freedom from constraint, to which the Greek term (*soterios*) adds wholeness. "He has sent me to proclaim freedom for the prisoner," Jesus consequently observed, "and recovery of sight for the blind" (Luke 4:18).

Here deliverance is set forth in the course of salvation history. God was active in times past with the patriarchs and prophets. He is about to take a giant step forward with the breaking in of a new age. The times were changing.

Salvation will be objectively realized before it is subjectively appropriated. The synoptic writers are agreed on this point (Luke 9:18-22; cf. Matt. 16:13-23; Mark 8:26-33). Deliverance would come by way of Jesus' vicarious death and triumphant resurrection.

From Jesus' vicarious death we reap gratuitous forgiveness. This significant authorial emphasis is found in key places throughout Luke-Acts. We discover it in the summary of John the Baptist's message in Luke 3:3, and in both Jesus' sermonic summary of His mission (4:18) and His great commission (24:47). "It is also found in the conclusion of the introductory sermon of Acts (2:38), in the explanation of God's having accepted the Gentiles apart from circumcision (Acts 10:43), in Paul's defense before Agrippa (26:18), and in two other sermons in Acts (5:31; 13:38)."[2]

John could not save persons. (No mere mortal could.) He called on people to repent in anticipation of the One to come. "John's baptism was a baptism of repentance," Paul recalls. "He told the people to believe in the one coming after him, that is, in Jesus" (Acts 19:4).

(2) When some men carrying a paralytic were unable to push their way through the crowd, they lowered him through a roof into Jesus' presence. "When Jesus saw their faith, he said: 'Friend, your sins are forgiven'" (Luke 5:20). This curious text has given rise to speculation concerning the possibility of *vicarious faith*, whether in fact persons can exercise faith on behalf of others.

Several comments seem in order. First, this account would apart from reference to the forgiveness of sins appear as simply another miracle story. Jesus characteristically healed in response to faith, whether individual or pervasive. In this manner, He gave evidence of his messianic calling.

Second, Luke would probably take this as a healing precedent for church ministry. "Is any one of you sick?" James inquired. "He should call the elders of the church to pray over him and anoint him with oil in the name of the Lord. And the prayer offered in faith will make the sick person well, the Lord will raise him up" (James 5:14-15).

Third, such episodes sometimes give the impression of salvation parables. Jesus' healing of blind Bartimaeus is a classic case in point (Luke 18:35-43). "Receive your sight," Jesus responded, "your faith has healed you." After this, he followed the Master, as would a disciple. Luke, by excluding Mark's elaboration *along the road* (9:52) heightens the parabolic potential.

Fourth, Jesus indicates that He has power not only to heal but to forgive sins in response to faith.

> This included the faith both of the paralytic and his companions. This faith in the original setting would have been a faith in Jesus as one come from God who could heal. For Luke and his readers this would have involved a greater understanding of who Jesus is and would have involved faith in him as the risen Lord.[3]

Finally, *faith* disclosed in the above manner implies a personal trust in Jesus. This expresses itself first concerning His healing ministry, and eventually as the guardian of our eternal destiny. Luke enjoys building bridges for his readers from the former to the latter.

(3) An expert of the law decided to test Jesus. "Teacher," he inquired, "what must I do to inherit eternal life?" (Luke 10:25). (Luke uses *eternal life* as synonymous with *salvation*, as can be seen from Luke 18:18, 30; Acts 13:46, 48.) "What is written in the Law?" Jesus replied. "Love the Lord your God with all your heart and with all your soul and with all your strength and with all your mind" he responded. With this, love your neighbor as yourself. "You have answered correctly," Jesus commended him. "Do this and you will live."

"If you want a way of salvation by doing, this is it. It is perhaps more likely that it is a repudiation of works. ...If we really love God in the way of which Jesus speaks, then we rely on him, nor ourselves."[4] Love God and do what you want, for in loving God you will do as He wishes.

Wishing to justify himself, the man continued. "Who is my neighbor?" he inquired. Jesus did not answer directly, but by way of a story. A man was traveling from Jerusalem to Jericho, and fell prey to thieves. Some time later, a priest happened by and saw the beaten man lying by the roadside. He passed by on the other side. So also a Levite. Conversely, a Samaritan stopped and cared for the injured man.

"Which of these three do you think was a neighbor to the man who fell into the hands of robbers?" Jesus asked. The expert replied: "The one who had mercy on him." Jesus thereupon concluded with an exhortation: "Go and do likewise."

While strictly speaking, Jesus' story speaks more explicitly to *who is my neighbor* than *how may I inherit eternal life*, the former is an extension of the latter. In retrospect, the man appears interested in religious casuistry. Jesus, on the other hand, turned the discussion to practical matters. We embrace salvation not in retreat from but in pursuit of responsibility for others.

(4) They crucified Jesus between two criminals. "Jesus," one of them plead, "remember me when you come into your kingdom" (Luke 23:42). Jesus confidently assured him: "I tell you the truth, today you will be with me in paradise." The hour was late, but the occasion opportune.

In this exchange between Jesus and the penitent, Luke records

> an act of salvation in a situation in which the word "save" has been used in taunts and ridicule. Three times he has been mocked with "Save yourself," the lone criminal adding "and us." Here Jesus does save someone, and that the one saved is a dying criminal is totally congenial to the types of persons blessed by Jesus through his ministry.[5]

As Jesus characterized His ministry, "For the Son of Man has come to seek and to save what was lost." (Luke 19:10).

Luke employs *into your kingdom* as equivalent to *salvation* and *eternal life*. Only the accent differs. *Into your kingdom* emphasizes salvation with regard to achieving God's benevolent purpose. The criminal yields in humble submission.

The contrasts are also worth noting. "Remember me *when* you come into your kingdom," the penitent plead. "*Today* you will be with me in paradise," Jesus replied. *When* was *now*. As Paul would subsequently state the matter, "now is the time of God's favor, now is the day of salvation" (2 Cor. 6:2).

Into your kingdom stands over against *in paradise*. While the former, as noted above, implies submission, the latter accents reward. Jesus thereby encouraged the man to anticipate a refreshing garden at the end of a wilderness journey.

(5) With the coming of the Holy Spirit, Peter was asked for instruction. Whereupon, he counseled: "Repent and be baptized, everyone of you, in the name of Jesus Christ so that your sins may be forgiven. And you will receive the gift of the Holy Spirit" (Acts 2:38). Those who accepted his guidance were baptized, and about three thousand were added to the faith community that day.

Salvation thus appears in context of the descent of the Holy Spirit. *Repentance* and *faith*, as related to the Pentecost event, resemble two sides of a coin. This can be seen from their setting, where the admonition to repent and acceptance leading to baptism appear in parallel construction. Those who repent believe, and those who believe repent.

Baptism suggests four corollaries. First, as relates to repentance/faith. "Baptism is the concrete expression of the moral choice that has been made. It vividly portrays in time and space the inner decision made by the participant. ...For one participating, it was really a drama of decision!"[6]

Second, as concerns forgiveness. As John's baptism expressed forgiveness,

> symbolized in the act of washing, so too Christian baptism was regarded as a sign of forgiveness. But Christian baptism conveyed an additional blessing. John had said that he baptized (only) with water but the Messiah would baptize with the Holy Spirit, and this gift accompanies water-baptism performed by the church in the name of Jesus.[7]

Third, as regards the vicarious nature of salvation. "We were therefore buried with him through baptism into death in order that, just as Christ was raised from the dead through the glory of the Father, we too may live a new life" (Rom. 6:4). Of similar intent, "For as in Adam all die, so in Christ all will be made alive" (1 Cor. 15:22).

Finally, as witness to the indwelling Spirit. It is an outward confession of an inward transformation.

It would already appear that the more salvation formulae change, the more the central meaning remains constant. Salvation history runs true to form.

(6) A crowd gathered at the temple gate to view the cripple who had been healed. Peter used this occasion to appeal to those assembled: "Repent then, and turn to God, so that your sins may be wiped out, that times of refreshing may come from the Lord, and that he may send the Christ" (Acts 3:19). Indeed, all the prophets have foretold these things that God has brought to pass.

The precise relation of *conversion* (*epistrophe*) to *repentance* has been variously understood. It implies, in any case, a turning about. The prodigal sets his face toward home. The far country is at his back.

Something of this turn about is already implied in *repentance*. To repent is not simply to wallow in self-pity. It is to reach out for help. Or as sometimes stated, it implies *godly sorrow*.

That your sins may be wiped out appears interchangeable with *forgiveness.* *Forgiveness*, thus understood, is not partial but complete. As with Isaiah, "though your sins are like scarlet, they shall be as white as snow; though they are red as crimson, they shall be like wool" (1:18).

Peter deftly focuses their attention on the return of Christ. No doubt they shared with the apostles a concern for the restoration (Acts 1:6). Peter observes that they compound the problem by rejecting God's Anointed. This, he graciously allows, was done through ignorance.

Now that God has brought to pass what was foretold, the apostle urges those gathered around him to repent. Paul followed a similar line of reasoning with his Athenian audience: "In the past God overlooked such ignorance, but now he commands all people everywhere to repent" (Acts 17:30). *This* is the day of salvation. It calls for a *decision*. We put ourselves at grave risk by procrastinating.

(7) When brought before the Sanhedrin to give account for the apostles' teaching, Peter remonstrated: "Salvation is to be found in no one else, for there is no other name under heaven given to men by which we must be saved" (Acts 4:12).

As earlier mentioned, a healing narrative can serve in parabolic fashion. "It was Jesus, then, who *saved* the lame man. Peter claims that only Jesus can offer salvation in the fullest sense; his is the only name which has received power from God to give salvation to men."[8]

The name stands for the person. It reveals Jesus' identity as Savior. It also introduces His saving work. "She will give birth to a son, and you are to give him the name Jesus," the angel announced to Joseph, "because he will save his people from their sins" (Matt. 1:21).

Two principles appear involved in this remarkable claim. First, God takes the initiative to reveal Himself. Man's initiative *exchanges the glory of the immortal God* for images drawn from creation. Persisting in his waywardness, he not only falls into grievous sin, but approves those who do so (Rom. 1:23, 29-32). Thus he remains unless God should restore him.

Second, only God saves. Man cannot help himself in whole or in part. He can only rely on God's mercy.

> This is the "scandal of particularity." In one particular person and event, God has overcome the relativizing conditions of history; in one event God has offered a truth and a grace found nowhere else, on which the salvation of the world hinges. If God is God, this is possible.[9]

Since God *is* God, Peter with Luke's obvious approval assures us that this is true.

(8) Paul in defense of Gentile freedom observed: "He (God) made no distinction between us and them, for he purified their hearts by faith. ...We believe it is through the grace of our Lord Jesus that we are saved, just as they are" (Acts 15:9, 11). His insistence eventually won the support of the Jerusalem Council over the objections of his opposition.

Here we encounter the apostle's characteristic emphases on *faith* and *grace*. "The experience whereby man appropriates to himself the effects of the Christ-event is for Paul faith (*pistis*). This experience begins with the hearing of the 'word' about Christ and ends in a personal commitment of the whole man to his person and revelation."[10] It begins as hearing and ends in obedience.

> This faith of the Christian is a gift of God just as the whole salvic process is. ...Since God accosts a man as a responsible person, he is free to accept or reject that gracious call. And faith is but the acceptance of the response on the part of man who realizes that the whole initiative rests with God.[11]

"Therefore," Paul concludes, "the promise comes by faith, so that it may be by grace and may be guaranteed to all Abraham's offspring--not only to those who are of the law but also to those who are of the faith of Abraham" (Rom. 4:16).

There is one thing further to consider. Paul submits as evidence of Gentile salvation the fact that they too have received the Holy Spirit (15:8). This reminds us that whereas man looks on the outward appearance, God sees the heart. "For it is with your heart that you believe and are justified, and it is with your mouth that you confess and are saved" (Rom. 10:10).

By way of extrapolation, this rules out cultural colonialism: the effort to make others conform to our predilections. It commends diversity constructively and creatively expressed. It also helps us get our priorities in order.

(9) We read of Lydia that the "Lord opened her heart to respond to Paul's message. When she and the members of her household were baptized, she invited us to her home" (Acts 16:14-15). Her offer of hospitality was accepted.

Luke notes that Lydia was a *Godfearer*. This may be understood in a generalized or specialized sense: as one who reverences God or a Gentile that worships at the synagogue. In either case, it implies that she was earnestly seeking God's will for her life. "Seek first his kingdom and his righteousness," Jesus admonished, "and all these things will be given to you as well" (Matt. 6:33).

The imperfect tense suggests that she either heard Paul on more than one occasion or over a period of time. She was weighing matters carefully. She was not inclined to let credulity substitute for faith.

Lydia along with her household responded affirmatively. We naturally wonder who were likely implicated by *the members of her household.*

> In the story all of the information centers around Lydia and the women; her vocation as described and her home background is given. ...The best suggestion would be those associated with her as assistants in her vocational pursuits: bond servants or slave, hired assistants, business associates.[12]

Acts records three other instances concerning households: with Cornelius (10:23-48; 11:14), the Philippian jailor (16:3-34), and Crispus (18:8). Each of these present a different exegetical challenge, but we will explore the matter no further.

We will instead finish off on a practical note, as Luke is want to do. Salvation expresses itself with Lydia offering hospitality. An open hand symbolizes salvation better than a closed fist. Like Jesus, the disciple is called not to be served but to serve others.

(10) When given a hearing by Agrippa, Paul responded: "First to those in Jerusalem and in all Judea, and to the Gentiles also, I preached that they should repent and turn to God and prove their repentance by their deeds" (Acts 26:20). Agrippa remained unconvinced. Paul was adamant: "I pray God that not only you but all who are listening to me today may become as I am, except for these chains."

Paul herein touches on three aspects of his ministry: his preaching of repentance, conversion, and demonstration. *Repentance,* all things considered, appears as the most resilient factor in the salvation formulae. Time and again we are reminded of the need to repudiate our prodigal behavior. Jesus means to save us not *in* but *from* our sin.

Conversion, as we have seen, suggests a turn about. As such, it is a more general phenomenon than experienced in Christian context. Such occurs in everyday life, with or without religious motivation. What makes Christian conversion unique is the Christ factor. The *sin qua non* is Christ.

"Show me your faith without deeds," James writes, "and I will show you my faith by what I do" (2:18). Paul would agree that faith rightly so called should be expressed in doing good. Donald Bloesch comments:

The gospel apart from the law becomes cheap grace. It then promotes not the righteousness of God but antinomianism. The law apart from the gospel issues in works-righteousness or legalism. It also subverts the righteousness of faith that alone saves from sin.[13]

"I was not disobedient to the vision from heaven," Paul observes. Even so, he adds: "I am saying nothing beyond what the prophets and Moses said would happen--that the Christ would suffer and, as the first to rise from the dead would proclaim light to his own people and to the Gentiles."

Our faith is directed not simply to the mystical presence of Christ or to the unconditional, but to Jesus Christ crucified and risen according to the Scriptures. The act of believing (*fides qua creditur*), though supremely important, must never prevail over the content of faith (*fides quae creditur*).[14]

In Summary

We have, as it were, been looking at some of the standing trees. It remains to make out the contours of the forest.

Scripture emphasizes the importance of *salvation* in various ways. Once, after Jesus' disciples returned from a successful ministry, He cautioned them: "Do not rejoice that the spirits submit to you, but rejoice that your names are written in heaven" (Luke 10:20). On another occasion, He inquired: "What good is it for a man to gain the whole world, and lose his soul?" (Mark 8:37).

Given the focus of Luke's two volume work on the universal offer of salvation, this seemed a likely source to explore. Out of fifty-six inviting passages, we considered ten for the purposes of this paper. Our criteria for selection was representative character and/or some distinctive feature.

I had not expected to discover so great a diversity in salvation formulae. An approximate count yielded thirty-six variations. Upon further reflection, these seemed to derive from different perspectives, narrative relevance, effort to economize, and personal preference. Luke takes all this in stride, as if to applaud the effort.

Reflecting still further, Luke seems to inter-phase three fundamental perspectives concerning salvation. We may refer to these as *historical*, *theological*, and *existential*. They jostle among themselves to gain position.

The *historical* perspective is most striking for its ambiguity. Events may be interpreted in one way or another. Since this is the case, Gamaliel urged the Jewish authorities to free the apostles. "For if their purpose or activity is of human origin, it will fail," he reasoned. "But if it is from God, you will not be able to stop these men; you will only find yourselves fighting against God" (Acts 5:38-39).

In another context, I commented:

> We do well to allow God the prerogative of transcendence and to accept the ambiguity that results. One God is enough; we do not have to know everything about everything. God has revealed what is essential for our well-being, and we can trust Him for the rest.[15]

Luke seems to imply as much.

The *theological* perspective provides us with God's commentary on events. "These men are not drunk, as you suppose," Peter speaks as one sent by God (i.e., an apostle). In the last days, he explains, God would pour out His Spirit on all people.

What God reveals reminds us of how much we still have to learn. "For we know in part and we prophesy in part," Paul allowed, "but when perfection comes, the imperfect disappears" (1 Cor. 13:9).

The *existential* perspective sees salvation from *within* as opposed to the *historical*, and from *below* in contrast to the *theological*. It is salvation as we experience it and bear witness of it.

It implies a climactic decision, repentance and faith, the experience of forgiveness, grace abounding, power invigorating, fruitfulness, and constant vigilance. It reminds us of John Bunyan's celebrated allegory *Pilgrim's Progress*. In captivating style, he recounts how pilgrim makes his way to the celestial city. The road sign would read: SALVATION.

Editorial note. In the above connection, we struggled for theological precision with regard to *salvation*. With what follows, we suggest that imprecision sometimes better serves as we attempt to understand and appreciate our place in God's world. In the latter regard, we enlist the help of *fuzzy set theory.*

ENDNOTES

1. Morris Inch, "Interpreting Luke-Acts," *The Literature and Meaning of Scripture* (Inch and Bullock, eds.), p. 127.
2. Robert Stein, *Luke*, p. 101.
3. Ibid., p. 176.
4. Leon Morris, *Luke*, p. 206.
5. Fred Craddock, *Luke*, p. 273.
6. Oscar Brooks, *The Drama of Decision*, p. 31.
7. I. Howard Marshall, *Acts*, p. 81.
8. Ibid., p. 100.
9. Paul Knitter, *No Other Name?*, p. 89.
10. Joseph Fitzmyer, *Pauline Theology*, p. 64.
11. Ibid., pp. 64-65.
12. Brooks, *op. cit.*, p. 62.
13. Donald Bloesch, *Freedom For Obedience*, p. 132.
14. Donald Bloesch, *Essentials of Evangelical Theology*, Vol. 1, p. 2.
15. Morris Inch, *My Servant Job*, p. 48.

BIBLIOGRAPHY

Bloesch, Donald. *Essentials of Evangelical Theology*. Three volumes. San Francisco: Harper & Row, 1978.

_____. *Freedom For Obedience*. San Francisco: Harper & Row, 1987.

Brooks, Oscar. *The Drama of Decision*. Peabody: Hendrickson, 1987.

Craddock, Fred. *Luke*. Louisville: John Knox, 1990.

Fitzmyer, Joseph. *Pauline Theology*. Englewood Cliffs: Prentice-Hall, 1967.

Inch, Morris. "Interpreting Luke-Acts," *The Literature and Meaning of Scripture* (Inch and Bullock, eds), 173-189.

_____ and C. Hassell Bullock, eds. *The Literature and Meaning of Scripture*. Grand Rapids: Baker, 1981.

_____. *My Servant Job*. Grand Rapids: Baker, 1979.

Knitter, Paul. *No Other Name?* Maryknoll: Orbis, 1986.

Marshall, I. Howard. *Acts*. Grand Rapids: Eerdmans, 1991.

Morris, Leon. *Luke*. Grand Rapids: Eerdmans, 1990.

Stein, Robert. *Luke*. Nashville: Broadman, 1992.

FUZZY SET THEOLOGY

Theology should by all means be precise. So conventional wisdom has assured us, and so we have been led to believe. As for justification, we have invoked the notion of theology as science. It, nevertheless, now appears that this appeal may undermine the purpose for which it was intended.

George Klir and Bo Yaun explain as follows:

> Among the various paradigmatic changes in science and mathematics in this century, one such change concerns the concept of *uncertainty*. In science, this change has been manifested by a gradual transition from the traditional view, which insists that uncertainty is undesirable in science and should be avoided by all possible means, to an alternative view, which is tolerant of uncertainty and insists that science cannot avoid it.[1]

With this in mind, we return to our theological drawing board.

Fuzzy Phenomena

We will, however, postpone our return for a brief excursion into the realm of fuzzy logic. "Fuzzy concepts derive from fuzzy phenomena that commonly occur in the natural world."[2] For example, *rain* is a natural phenomenon that is difficult to describe precisely, since it occurs with varied intensity. We struggle to make our description more definite by distinguishing among light, moderate, and heavy rain. Still, it is difficult to say what constitutes *light, moderate*, and *heavy*. Even if we were to do so, most of us would not have the means to measure whether rain conforms to our categorical standards.

Rather than necessarily defeat our purposes, fuzzy logic can significantly further them. "The human brain has the incredible ability of processing fuzzy classification, fuzzy judgment, and fuzzy reasoning. The natural languages are ingeniously permeated with inherent fuzziness so that we can express such information content in a few words."[3]

As a result, we can manage uncertainties, deal with our problems in a more comprehensive fashion, and make use of common sense reasoning. For instance, suppose one wants to give directions to the person driving an automobile. Even if the former knew within a centimeter the distance to the next turn-off, the latter could make no sense of the data. Instead, a simple warning that we are approaching the turn will not only suffice, but be more intelligible than distance given in centimeters.

All things considered, fuzzy logic seems especially appropriate to human concerns. Martin Brown and Chris Harris comment in this connection: "As the complexity of a system increases and our ability to make precise and yet significant statements about its behavior diminishes until a threshold is reached beyond which precision and significance become almost mutually exclusive characteristics."[4] This being so, they conclude that the *humane* thing to do would be to use *soft* (imprecise) information.

Illustrative of this thesis, *good* people characteristically have faults, and *bad* persons sometimes do commendable things. Fuzzy logic therefore helps us cope with the Biblical narrative, where persons are realistically portrayed.

This observation would seem to invite us to get on with the topic as announced. We will look at five examples; two each from Biblical and systematic theology, and one from historical theology. Thereafter, we will draw some preliminary conclusions.

Cases In Point

First set, first example. We read from the Genesis account: "Now the earth was formless and empty, darkness was over the surface of the deep, and the Spirit of God was hovering over the waters" (Gen. 1:2). "As we move beyond v. 1 and into v. 2, we do not, unfortunately, leave behind all problems of translation and interpretation. As will shortly become evident, v. 2 bristles with points of debate."[5] So *precision logic* would dictate. *Fuzzy logic* conversely would encourage us to settle for something less problematic.

Victor Hamilton nevertheless launches into an extended discussion of the alternative translations *the Spirit of God, the spirit of God, a wind of God,* and *an awesome gale.* Characteristic of his general discussion, he submits three objections to the last of these options. One will suffice to illustrate his overriding concern for precision:

Second, it is true that there are some plausible examples in the Hebrew Bible of *elohim* used as a superlative, that is, as an attributive adjective rather than a noun. But even these examples are ambiguous. Thus, in Gen. 23:6, is Abraham addressed as "a prince of God" or as "a mighty prince"? (Other examples follow.) But even if the translation were transparent in these three references, this would not allow one to apply the same force to *elohim* in Gen. 1:2c, for two reasons. First, how could the reader of the original or the translator be expected to differentiate the *elohim* of v. 2c from all other occurrences of *elohim* in the first chapter? Second, taking *elohim* as superlative, and as a further descriptive part of the chaos of formlessness and darkness, places *elohim* in v. 2c in opposition to the *elohim* who in v. 1 creates the heaven and the earth, and who in v. 3 speaks.[6]

Two pages later, Hamilton has managed to dismiss two of the four options, but raises in their stead a variety of related questions: "But does the contents of v. 2 describe something that came to be after God created an original perfect universe? Or does v. 2 expand on and clarify the shape of the earth when God first created it? Or does v. 2 describe the situation before God begins his actual creation as introduced in v. 3?"[7] These questions require an additional two pages for him to negotiate.

As a result, Hamilton concludes that verse 2 describes the situation prior to the detailed creation that follows. As a matter of fact, his conclusion may have resulted more from common sense than detailed deliberation.

Fuzzy thinking, in contrast to *precision thinking*, is more tolerant of uncertainty. It might consequently be satisfied with noting the apparent similarity between the Genesis narrative and other High God traditions. More in particular and as relates to verse 2, the celestial Potter casts His clay before creating a vessel for use. Or, as in an alternative instance, He selects a suitable piece of wood before carving a preconceived figure. In either case, primeval chaos appears as if an initial step in the creative process.

As for *the Spirit of God hovering over the waters*, so God momentarily pauses before His extended activity. No further explanation appears required, nor would it seem to serve any constructive purpose.

First set, second example. While Jesus and His disciples were eating, the former took bread, and having given thanks, broke it and gave it to the latter. "Take and eat," Jesus urged them, "this is my body" (Matt. 26:26).

Then he took the cup, gave thanks and offered it to them, saying, "Drink from it, all of you. This is the blood of the covenant, which is poured out for many for the forgiveness of sins. I tell you, I will not drink of this fruit of the vine from now on until that day when I drink it anew with you in my Father's kingdom" (vv. 27-30).

Marvin Wilson reconstructs the order of events as follows:

Whatever chronology of the Last Supper one adopts, it seems clear that Jesus instituted the Lord's Supper by associating it with the third cup of wine, which came after the Passover meal was eaten (cf. 1 Cor. 11:25). It was known as the "cup of redemption," which rabbinic tradition linked to the fourfold promise of redemption in Exodus 6:6-7: "I will redeem you".[8]

With this, Wilson supposes to paint with broad brush strokes.

"The unfinished meal of Jesus was a pledge that redemption would be consummated at that future messianic banquet when he takes the cup and 'drinks it anew in the kingdom of God' (Mark 14:25; cf. Matt. 26:29; Rev. 3:20; 19:6-9)."[9] We are thereby alerted to the *now but not yet* feature of Jesus' eschatology. Redemption is now available, but the consummation remains future. Once again, he paints with broad strokes.

The above seems illustrative of *fuzzy logic* in that it resembles the tip of the proverbial iceberg. It does not probe the murky waters below the surface.

Unimpressed, others have attempted to explain precisely what Jesus meant by declaring that this was His body and blood. This gave rise to four interpretations along with various refinements: that the elements are actually transformed into Christ's body and blood, that the former contain the latter, that the former spiritually convey the latter, and that the former represent the latter.

Even so, Millard Erickson reminds us that there are points of general consensus (allowing for the uncertainty principle). Among these are that it was established by Christ, meant to be repeated, was a form of proclamation, was of spiritual benefit to the partaker, is restricted to the followers of Jesus, and takes place in community.[10] These, it would appear, result not from *precision* but *fuzzy thinking*.

All this brings to mind an experience Moshe Rosen, founder of *Jews for Jesus*, shared some years ago. It seems that he was visiting a church for what was perhaps his first time. Reading through the bulletin, he came to a reference to *communion*. It sounded like *communism* to him. Singling out an usher standing nearby, he called the fellow over. "What is *communion*?" Rosen wanted to know. "I'll tell you after the service," the other replied. "If I'd wanted to know after the service," Rosen responded, "I'd have asked you after the service."

Whereupon, he received an abbreviated explanation. This, in turn, called his attention to the front of the sanctuary. There he observed linens laid out as if to cover a body. "Of course," he assured us, " I didn't think that it was an actual person. We Jews are fond of object lessons, and I supposed this to be one of them." He was content not to press the matter further, much to the relief of the embarrassed usher.

Second set, third example. Our best theological minds have over the years struggled to reconcile determinism/grace with free will. Consequently, our conscientious seminary professor outlined perhaps ten alternatives. Three or four of them subsequently survived the rigor of precise analysis, before we felt justified in moving on to more manageable concerns.

Donald Bloesch would seem to conclude that the topic may not demand this kind of scrutiny. He comments as follows:

> In our historical analysis of the controversy over grace and free will we did not intend to suggest that the truth lies exclusively on one side. Synergism is of course a real danger, but we must also recognize the complementary danger of monergism in which God is portrayed as the sole actor in our salvation. ...He is the sole efficient cause of salvation but not the only causal factor in salvation. There are also secondary or instrumental causes that have to be taken into account.[11]

Lest we miss the point, he further explains:

> What is necessary to understand is that the act of salvation is a paradox or mystery which defies and eludes rational comprehension. The lapses into synergism and monergism can be accounted for by the ever-recurring attempts to resolve the paradox of salvation into a rationally understandable formula.[12]

We note in passing the theological tradition concerning *paradox* within which Bloesch addresses the issue. First, it concerns *logical* rather than *rhetorical paradox*. The former has substance, whereas the latter serves simply as a figure of speech.

Second, *logical paradox* arises from the attempt to correlate diverse and seemingly contradictory data. Such effort is inhibited not only by our finite condition but human perversity.

Third, two differing interpretations of *logical paradox* emerge in the course of theological reflection. One asserts that paradox is actual, and the other that it is only apparent. Bloesch would seem to favor the latter alternative. In this connection, he applauds Jonathan Edwards' commentary: "In efficacious grace we are not merely passive, nor yet does God do some, and we do the rest. But God does all, and we do all. God produces all, and we act all... . God is the only proper author and fountain; we only are the proper actors."[13]

Fuzzy logic provides a promising alternative to *paradox* for managing complex and imprecise data. In addition, it has the advantage of being a commonly accepted *modus operandi*. It does not, on the other hand, appear as a questionable means of handling a theological conundrum.

With this in mind, we touch on a relevant text from Paul's epistle to the Ephesians: "For he chose us in him before the creation of the world" (1:4). A *fuzzy logic* interpretation should highlight two obvious concerns. First, "Christians need to realize that their faith rests completely on the work of God and not on the unsteady foundation of anything else. It is all the Lord's work, and in accordance with his plan, a plan that reaches back *before the foundation of the world*."[14] We have, for this reason, no cause for boasting.

Second, God's purpose extends beyond salvation to sanctification. He does not intend to leave the task uncompleted.

Does this preclude human cooperation? Decidedly not! Elsewhere Paul admonishes his readers: "...continue to work out your salvation with fear and trembling, for it is God who works in you to will and to act according to his good purpose" (Phil. 2:12).

Where does this leave us with regard to logic? "Classical logic deals with *propositions* that are required to be either *true* or *false*. Each proposition has an opposite, which is usually called a *negation* of the proposition."[15] This assumption has nevertheless been challenged from Aristotle on (cf. *On Interpretation*). With the advent of *fuzzy logic*, a third option appears: that of *indeterminacy*--as when we lack the proper means of measurement. Such would seem evident with regard to the determinism/grace and free will issue.

Second set, fourth example. We are singularly indebted to George Eldon Ladd for his comprehensive treatment of *The Kingdom of God*. He pursued the topic with unrelenting vigor, as if to expound the inexorable. "Modern scholarship," he concludes, "is quite unanimous in the opinion that the Kingdom of God was the central message of Jesus."[16]

Casting back, we discover *The Kingdom* in connection with the preaching of John the Baptist. Still further, we uncover it as God covenants with the chosen people. Over all, it persists regardless of circumstance as God's sovereign reign over creation and history.

Focusing on the emerging present, we encounter *The Kingdom* fleshed out in the life of Jesus. In addition, it is expressed in the form of an invitation to those who hear the good news. Moreover, its working proves to be quite mysterious. (*Mystery* like *paradox* may alert us to imprecision.) Ladd appropriately comments: "The Kingdom is working quietly, secretly among men. It does not force itself upon them; it must be willingly received. But wherever it is received, the word of the Kingdom, which is practically identical with the Kingdom itself, brings forth much fruit."[17]

As a result, there comes to be a people associated with God's working in the end times. Ladd states five cogent propositions concerning the intricate relationship between church and kingdom: (1) the church is not the kingdom, (2) the kingdom creates the church, (3) the church witnesses to the kingdom, (4) the church is the instrument of the kingdom, and (5) the church is the custodian of the kingdom.[18]

Seemingly overlooked in his discussion, we note the impact of Jesus outside of but not necessarily irrespective of the church. That is, as it relates to political, social, and cultural spin-offs. While more subtle in nature, these too bear witness to the breaking in of *The Kingdom*.

Looking to the future, we anticipate that *The Kingdom of God* will come in its fullness. Ladd embraces in this connection the model set forth by Geerhardus Vos and Oscar Cullmann, among others, that we live in what resembles an overlay of the present age and the age to come. We experience, as it were, a tension between the *now* and *not yet*. As such, Jurgen Moltmann reminds us that we are more drawn by the future than pushed by the past.

Shifting from *precision logic*, we pick up a distinction made by Norman Perrin some years ago concerning *The Kingdom*. *Tensive symbols*, according to Perrin, have a simple one-to-one correlation to what they represent. *Steno-symbols*, on the other hand, have "a set of meanings that can neither be exhausted nor adequately expressed by any one referent."[19] Or perhaps, from *fuzzy logic* perspective, any combination of referents. In any case, Perrin concluded that *The Kingdom of God* qualifies as an unmitigated *steno-symbol*.

In the above connection, *precision analysis* would seem to play a more restricted role than we might have imagined; in particular, it exposes for consideration certain referents to *The Kingdom*. In pressing beyond this point, it threatens to become reductionistic. Contrary to much conventional thinking, the *truth* does not always require that we force ever closer to the subject under consideration, but back off to appreciate its genuine complexity.

Fifth example. Martin Luther's struggle to discover assurance is common knowledge. After prolonged anguish, he focused on the text "the just shall live by faith" (Rom. 1:17), and this became his beacon light during the years to follow.

It also introduced a persisting controversy over the relationship between faith and good works. He addressed the topic early on with *A Treatise on Good Works.* Herein, he cogently writes:

> We ought first to know that there are no good works except those which God has commanded, even as there is no sin except that which God has forbidden. Therefore whoever wishes to know and to do good works needs nothing else than to know God's commandments.[18]

After this, he points out that *the first and highest,* and *the most precious of all* good works is faith in Christ. Luther fervently elaborates:

> So a Christian who lives in this confidence toward God, knows all things, can do all things, undertakes all things that are to be done, and does everything cheerfully and freely; not that he may gather many merits and good works, but because it is a pleasure for him to please God thereby.[21]

Whereupon, he set out to refine the matter ever more precisely. Fundamental to his thinking was the distinction between *the works of the law* and *the works of faith.* The former consists, not with matters of substance, but what we do solely on the urging of the law (through fear or promise of reward).

Conversely, the latter are such as are generated from our liberty in Christ, and our love of God. As Luther puts it, God does not accept the person because of his works but the works because of the person.

Not all works, however, fall into the above categories. There are *preparatory works.* These resemble *the works of the law* in that they do follow from faith. On the other hand, they resemble *the works of faith* with regard to intent. They are, in a qualified sense, righteous works because they exhibit a will to be righteous.

While we have little more than scratched the surface, it should already be evident to what lengths Luther was prepared to go in order to promote his theological agenda with regard to faith/works. Time and occasion would allow him to press his thesis, and in the process attempt to demolish the position of his opponents.

As for the latter, they held out for what is sometimes described as Semi-Pelagianism. Pelagius was a zealous ascetic, who emphasized man's uninhibited free will and moral responsibilities. Qualifications aside, he believed that what God required of man, man was capable of doing. Otherwise promoted, God extends grace equally to all.

Thus the lines were drawn, with the controversy continuing unabated to the present, although it often yields more heat than light. *Controversy*, as with *paradox* and *mystery*, may suggest the natural limitations of *precision logic*. That is, we attempt in vain to simplify what is by nature complex and complicated.

Dietrich Bonhoeffer, who stood appreciatively within the Lutheran tradition, introduced what might qualify as an example of *fuzzy logic*. As he saw the matter, *those who believe obey, and those who obey believe*. As sometimes put, our concern is not with *faith and works*, but *a faith that works*.

Is there a place for *precision logic* in theological reflection? Bonhoeffer would certainly answer in the affirmative. Is its legitimate role limited so that we may profit from the assistance of *fuzzy logic*? If actions can speak for words, then Bonhoeffer would again agree.

In Summary and Anticipation

What conclusions can be drawn concerning the above cases in point? By way of response, we introduce the following set of propositions.

1. As noted at the outset, theology has been characteristically indebted to *precision logic*. We assume, even when not made explicit, that success lies in exacting definition. Anything less would be to admit a lack of expertise resulting in projected failure.

This reaps two immediate results. First, it determines in large measure our theological agenda. Second, it establishes how we will work through that agenda. Whether in the former or latter connection, we are held captive by the methodology we select. As sometimes put, choice reenters as control.

2. The problem has not gone unnoticed, as evidenced by such theological devices as *paradox* and *mystery*. These, along with *controversy* resulting from our theological disputations, remind us (as stated earlier) both of the limitations of our reason and perversity of our disposition.

3. In defense of *precision logic*, theology has appealed to science for precedence. What presumably worked well in the latter instance should, qualifications aside, work well with the former. As a result, theology

hoped to achieve an objectivity otherwise missing.

The line of reasoning is clearly suspect. The scientific method succeeds only insofar as our data can be carefully regulated. In contrast and by way of protest, William Roweton observes:

> Educational psychology is misdirected, for researchers have inherited a simplistic and distortive model of man. ...Child learning and development is considerably more individually variant, relativistic, and erratic, and apparently unpredictable than commonly approved methodology would ever permit.[22]

A similar complaint could be registered on behalf of theology, and in connection with complex variables.

4. Even were the conclusion not suspect, science has subsequently introduced *fuzzy logic* as a means for handling complex reality. As such, it takes on the character of a *paradigm shift*. A *paradigm* is "a set of theories, standards, principles, and methods that are taken for granted by the scientific community in a given field."[23] Employing this concept, Thomas Kuhn (*The Structure of Scientific Revolutions*) "characterizes scientific development as a process in which periods of *normal science*, based on a particular paradigm, are interwoven with periods of paradigm shifts."[24]

Although differing in some particulars, *paradigm shifts* enjoy in common that (1) they are initiated via persisting problems, (2) each when introduced is repudiated in various ways (ignored, ridiculed, attacked, etc.) by most in a given field, (3) those in support are usually relatively young or new in the field, and do not exercise much leverage, (4) eventually headway is achieved on pragmatic grounds, and (5) as a rule, the larger its scope, the longer it requires to take hold.[25] If *fuzzy logic* runs true to its paradigmatic form, it will probably achieve a broad consensus with the passing of time.

5. A *paradigm shift* does not negate what is valid in a previous paradigm, but casts it in a more acceptable light. We would assume this would be the case with *precision logic*. As a matter of record, it serves us better in some regards than in others.

Meanwhile, *fuzzy logic* provides a needed balance. It allows us to manage complex situations with credible results. As a bonus, it lends itself to cross-disciplinary studies.

6. *Fuzzy logic* also restrains us from engaging in trivial pursuit. Which, in turn, brings to mind Jesus' criticism of the religious elite: "You give a tenth of your spices--mint, dill, and cummin. But you have

neglected the more important matters of the law--justice, mercy, and faithfulness" (Matt. 23:23).

Their fault lay in a meticulous attention to minutia, while ignoring more important concerns. *Fuzzy logic* might nip this problem in the bud, along with the religious hypocrisy that often attends it.

7. From a constructive point of view, *fuzzy logic* urges us to consider the larger picture. As an example, certain Pharisees inquired of Jesus: "Is it lawful for a man to divorce his wife for any and every reason?" (Matt. 19:3). They meant thereby to test Him with regard to a question they had debated endlessly and fruitlessly among themselves.

> The issue was not divorce itself, the right to which they took for granted, but rather the justifiable grounds for divorce. Would Jesus side with the school of Shammai, which allowed divorce only on the grounds of sexual immorality, or would he side with the school of Hillel, which sanctioned divorce on the most trivial grounds? [26]

"Haven't your read," Jesus asked by way of response, "that at the beginning the Creator made them male and female, and said, 'For this reason a man will leave his father and mother and be united to his wife, and the two shall be one flesh'?" He said this to remind them of the original purpose in marriage, and as the constant point of reference for further discussion. "Therefore what God had joined together," He concluded, "let man not separate."

8. Existentially, *fuzzy logic* helps us get on with living. Introspection can become incapacitating. If we wait until assured that our motives are quite unmixed, we will never get around to constructive action.

In keeping with this line of thought, Jesus inquired of Peter: "Simon son of John, do you truly love me more than these?" (John 21:15). Whatever *these* have reference to and in response to Peter's affirmative reply, Jesus enjoined him: "Feed my lambs." All else was incidental: including Peter's previous failure, his present situation, and what John might do.

9. Epistemologically, *fuzzy logic* would cultivate humility. In this connection, we recall Job's tragic experience. Once among the most privileged of persons, he encountered one painful reverse after another. Whereupon, he vigorously protested the supposed injustice in his tale of woes.

"Will the one who contends with the Almighty correct him?" God inquires as if in shocked disbelief (40:1). With this, God directs the patriarch's attention to more comprehensive concerns, complex constructions, and benevolent purposes. After this, Job contritely concludes: "Surely I spoke of things I did not understand, things too wonderful to know" (42:1).

10. Ethically, *fuzzy logic* turns our attention from the simple accumulation of knowledge to its profitable application (wisdom). As if to comment, Luke reports that an *expert in the law* stood up to put Jesus to a test. "Teacher," he asked, "what must I do to inherit eternal life?" (10:25).

"What is written in the Law?" Jesus replied. "How do you read it?" The expert answered: "Love the Lord your God with all your heart and with all your soul and with all your strength and with all your mind, and love your neighbor as yourself." "You have answered correctly," Jesus replied. "This do and you will live."

Whereupon, wishing to justify himself, he inquired further: "And who is my neighbor?"

> We have two questions, two good answers, and two men who agree. What else could one ask? All kinds of things are wrong. Asking questions for the purpose of gaining an advantage over another is not a kingdom exercise. Neither is asking questions with no intention of implementing the answers.[27]

On the other hand, asking questions in order to better serve others is most assuredly a kingdom exercise.

11. In conclusion, *fuzzy logic* seems in substantial measure a return to common sense reasoning, and such theological reflection as may be consistent with it. With such in view, we recall the comment of Albert Shanker, writing for the *New York Times*:

> I suppose we must rejoice in the fact that after millions of dollars of research we have finally reached the same conclusions which have always been held by ordinary men on the basis of common sense. The lesson to be learned from this seems to be clear--that in the absence of hard, really air-tight, scientific evidence, common sense is a far better guide in reaching education solutions than what has thus far gone on under the guise of educational research.[28]

As for theology, we ought not confound but communicate what Francis Schaeffer liked to refer to as *the really real*. This would seem to imply learning how to live in God's world, by His grace, and for His glory.

Editorial note. The preceding qualifies more as an *occasional paper* than most. As such, it addresses a concern that has troubled me since early on in my theological pilgrimage. It also provided a refreshing diversion from a prolonged study of chaos theory, which spawned not only *Chaos Paradigm: A Theological Exploration* (1998), but the final two essays in this collection.

ENDNOTES

1. George Klir and Bo Yanu, *Fuzzy Sets and Fuzzy Logic*, p. 1.
2. Hong Xing Li and Vincent Yen, *Fuzzy Sets and Fuzzy Decision-Making*, p. 1.
3. Ibid.
4. Martin Brown and Chris Harris, *Neurofuzzy Adaptive Modeling and Control*, p. 19.
5. Victor Hamilton, *The Book of Genesis: Chapters 1-17*, p. 108.
6. Ibid., p. 112.
7. Ibid., p. 115.
8. Marvin Wilson, *Our Father Abraham*, p. 246.
9. Ibid., p. 247.
10. Millard Erickson, *Christian Theology*, Vol. 3, pp. 1109-1112.
11. Donald Bloesch, *Essentials of Evangelical Theology*, Vol. 1, p. 201.
12. Ibid.
13. Ibid., p. 204 (cf. Jonathan Edwards, "Miscellaneous Remarks," *The Works of Jonathan Edwards*--Hickman, ed., Vol. 2, p. 557).
14. Francis Foulkes, *Ephesians*, p. 55.
15. George Klir and Tina Folger, *Fuzzy Sets, Uncertainty, and Information*, p. 22.
16. George Eldon Ladd, *A Theology of the New Testament*, p. 57.
17. Ibid., p. 95.
18. Ibid., pp. 111-119.
19. Norman Perrin, *The Kingdom of God in the Teaching of Jesus*, p. 33.
20. Martin Luther, *A Treatise on Good Works*, I.1.
21. Ibid., I.6.
22. William Roweton, The Putative Effects of Educational Research," *Revitalizing Educational Psychology* (Roweton, ed.), p. 15.
23. Flir and Yuan, *op. cit.*, p. 30.
24. Ibid.
25. Ibid.
26. Donald Hagner, *Matthew 14-28*, p. 547.
27. Fred Craddock, *Luke*, p. 149.
28. Albert Shanker, *New York Times*, July 23, 1972 (quoted in William Roweton--ed., *Revitalizing Education Psychology*, p. 5).

BIBLIOGRAPHY

Bloesch, Donald. *Essentials of Evangelical Theology*, 2 vols. San Francisco: Harper & Row, 1978-1979.

Brown, Martin and Chris Harris. *Neurofuzzy Adaptive Modeling and Control.* New York: Prentice-Hall, 1994.

Craddock, Fred. *Luke.* Louisville: John Knox, 1990.

Erickson, Millard. *Christian Theology*, 3 vols. Grand Rapids: Baker, 1986.

Foulkes, Francis. *Ephesians.* Grand Rapids: Eerdmans, 1989.

Hagner, Donald. *Matthew 14-28.* Dallas: Word, 1995.

Hamilton, Victor. *The Book of Genesis: Chapters 1-17*, Grand Rapids: Eerdmans, 1990.

Klir, George and Tina Folger. *Fuzzy Sets, Uncertainty, and Information.* Englewood Cliffs: Prentice-Hall, 1988.

_____ and Bo Yaun. *Fuzzy Sets and Fuzzy Logic.* Upper Saddle River: Prentice-Hall, 1995.

Ladd, George Eldon. *A Theology of the New Testament.* Grand Rapids: Eerdmans, 1989.

Li, Hong Zing and Vincent Yen. *Fuzzy Sets and Fuzzy Decision-Making.* Boca Raton: CRC, 1995.

Luther, Martin. *A Treatise on Good Works.*

Perrin, Norman. *The Kingdom of God in the Teaching of Jesus.* Naperville: SCM, 1967.

Roweton, William. "The Putative Effects of Educational Research," *Revitalizing Educational Psychology* (Roweton, ed.), 11-16.

_____ (ed.). *Revitalizing Educational Psychology: Readings and Methods and Substance.* Chicago: Nelson-Hall, 1976.

Wilson, Marvin. *Our Father Abraham.* Grand Rapids: Eerdmans, 1989.

CHAOS AS THE CRUCIBLE
OF FAITH

"Always be prepared to give an answer to everyone who asks you to give the reason for the hope that you have" (1 Pet. 3:15). In such manner, Peter encouraged his readers to prime themselves to give a credible response for believing as they did. One ought not do less out of deference to self, others, and--above all--to the Almighty.

James Gleick, a prominent pioneer in chaos theory, subsequently comments: "An appreciation of chaos changes one's intuition about the world--one's sense of the orderly and disorderly possibilities lurking in any complex system."[1] If so and in keeping with the previous exhortation, it would seem proper that we explore the credibility of Christian faith from chaos perspective. We would hope in so doing to refine previous apologetic thinking, and perhaps gain new insights.

In particular, we will consider four related topics. First, chaos as a reality paradigm; second, theistic arguments re-visited; third, the experience of pain; finally, prospects of a paradigm shift. These, taken together, will serve as an initial consideration of the implications of chaos theory for Christian apologetics.

A Reality Paradigm

Seemingly without exception, theorists characterize chaos as a paradigm emerging from the real world. Ian Percival consequently observes: "Traditionally, scientists have looked for the simplest view of the world around us. Now, mathematics and computer power have produced a theory that helps researchers to understand the complexities of nature."[2] Some pages later, he concludes: "Understanding the subtle unfolding of chaos in a system is helping us to describe not only behavior of the floating leaf, the irregular heartbeat and the dripping tap, but many aspects of our complex Universe, on both a small and a grand scale."[3]

Peter Coveny wholeheartedly concurs: "The theory of chaos uncovers a new 'uncertainty principle' that governs how the real world behaves."[4] Coveney nonetheless adds a word of caution: "As physicists have already found through quantum mechanics, the full structure of the world is richer than our language can express and our brains comprehend."[4] As reminded by the apostle Paul, "we know in part" (1 Cor. 13:9).

Several questions come to mind. What is reality? What actually do we know of it? How do we improve on our understanding? What features are more important than others?

What is reality? *Reality* is what exists independent of volition; i.e., we cannot wish it away. As such, it may be objective or subjective. It could be out there, or in here.

What do we actually know of reality? We formulate our understanding of it through three stages: externalization, objectification, and internalization. *Externalization* refers to our involvement in the world, both in physical and cognitive fashion; *objectification* is the result of that activity as relates to what we perceive as external to ourselves; *internalization* results from how we consider our role within the scope of things. It is, from start to finish, a social process. It is, as with any human enterprise, fallible.

How do we improve on our understanding? First, by recognizing our limitations; second, by refining our insight; third, by making necessary alteration; fourth, by formulating new constructs. We thereby set out to creatively blend the best from our past with the promise of newly discovered information.

What are the priority concerns? "Actually, for scientists the more reliable a fact is, the more trivial and unimportant it becomes. For instance, the atomic weight of carbon can confidently be given as 12.111 atomic units. Yet this fact is basically just a curiosity... ."[6] It remains as such until worked into some meaningful context for humans in their individual and corporate enterprise.

Chaos theory is user-friendly to the social construction of reality. It grapples with life as we experience it (not as we would wish it to be); it provides data needed to construct our understanding of reality; it no less provides a corrective necessary in reality maintenance; it finally encourages us to press beyond the trivial to access our full potential as humans. Chaos thus fulfills our anticipation of being a real life paradigm.

It remains to appraise its apologetic significance. Negatively, it resists religious escapism. Positively, it encourages rigorous engagement. In both regards, it serves the gospel well.

Jacob Licht deliberately sets the scene:

> There are no dragons, ogres or enchanted palaces in it (Scripture), few
> great deeds of valour, no scorching love adventures, no richly
> embroidered plots. ...The ultimate theme of these narratives is, of course,
> the mighty deeds of God, but these remain most of the time in the
> background. The actual...subject matter is the lesser deeds of men.[7]

By way of elaboration, we first discover *events*. Some are ordinary,
some extraordinary. All alike are woven into God's redemptive design.

Events can be variously accounted for. John emphasizes the
miraculous as credentials confirming that Jesus was sent by God.
Conversely, those opposed attributed them to satanic powers. It remained
for a later generation to deny that they actually happened.

Those who contributed to the Biblical corpus assumed that these
events contributed to a fuller understanding of God and His ways in the
world. Here a little, there a little: each drew from the past and added in
anticipation of the future. It was from this precedent that Jewish
education set its course. For instance, a place would be set at the table for
Elijah. When the child inquired why this was done, his delighted parents
would explain that the prophet must come before the appearance of the
Messiah.

There are in the second place *people*. They are not as a rule bigger
than life. They in fact have feet of clay. David serves as a classic case in
point. Although uniquely favored, he committed grievous sin. Having
violated Bathsheba, he engineered the death of her husband.

Peter provides another example. One of Jesus' inner circle, he
continually solicited the Master's rebuke. He insisted that Jesus would not
go the way of the cross, argued concerning the washing of the disciples'
feet, impetuously cut off an ear of a servant of the high priest, and
eventually denied Jesus as predicted.

There were others. Most appear as callous and self-seeking. On the
other hand, some seem devout and responsible. Differences aside, all are
plagued by human frailties.

As for Jesus,

> He did not seem to them to be some indeterminate person from some
> halfway land in which human and divine were intermingled; he did not
> seem to them a kind of Greek demigod, neither fully human or fully
> divine; he did not seem to them so divine as to be inhuman.[8]

He did not seem so peculiar as not to be at home in the real world.

As a matter of fact, it was the *manner* of Jesus' teaching that first solicited attention. Rather than draw upon religious precedent, as was the custom, he taught with authority. With the passing of time, this authority issue would not be put to rest, but extended to embrace His person and ministry.

Jesus' departure was drawing near. "As the Father has sent me," He announced to the disciples, "I am sending you" (John 20:21). Not to some safe sanctuary, but to minister in a troubled world. Not to feather their own nest, but to meet the needs of others. Not through isolation from the world, but through engagement.

Christ and chaos join in chorus to invite us into the real world. Here we may discover a reason for being, a cause worthy of our potential, and grace sufficient for every challenge. If not here, then nowhere else.

Theistic Arguments Revisited

Such data as we derive from existence, we use to create a comprehensive view of reality. This world view, or symbolic universe, serves us in two ways. First, it helps us make sense out of the totality of our experience, and second, view our personal life as meaningful.

It is in the above context that we reconsider the traditional arguments for God's existence. They relate to human posturing in the world of sense experience, where chaos remains a constant threat and/or unique opportunity.

Cosmological argument. Thomas Aquinas reasoned that everything that happens has a cause, and this, in turn, has a cause; leading to an infinite cause--which we refer to as *God.* The argument is initially vulnerable from excluding the alternative of an infinite regression. The cause-effect relationship may also be explained otherwise: as simply a statistical probability, or humanly imposed structure on observable phenomena. In addition, a great gulf exists between speculation concerning a first cause and the portrait of God revealed in Scripture.

There are, of course, various ways of putting the cosmological argument. For instance, we

know from the fact that there was a time when a thing did not exist, that it might not have existed at all or existed differently. Everything points beyond itself to something else. Hence, there must have been a time when nothing existed. In this case, nothing could have come to exist, for there was no causal agency. Since things came to exist, there must have been a noncontingent cause, which we designate *God.*[9]

John Casti responds from chaos perspective:

> On the basis of the various explanations put forward for the emergence of life here on Earth, my impression is that should the Earth be wiped clean of all life today in some kind of planetary Armageddon, the likelihood of life forms of any kind reemerging in a few billion years would be a bet that not even Lloyd's of London would put on the board.[10]

He concludes from this that there is something very special about life in general, and human life in particular. The *something special* may be attributed to the existence of God.

Casti exercises restraint in this connection. With what effect, we can only surmise. As a matter of fact, understatement often proves to be the most effective form of an argument.

On the other hand, the answers we introduce to explain the origin of life often do not answer. As an example, we say that life may have come from some extra-terrestrial source. That is not a final solution, for we then have to ask where that life came from, and find ourselves back in a cosmological regression.

Chaos theory reminds us the theistic arguments serve as probability considerations, but we ought to have known that previously. It moreover assures us that probability arguments are proper, especially given the complex (nonlinear) character of reality. That is something we need to bear in mind. Our human agenda, all things considered, should be to make sense of life as a whole, and our individual roles within it.

Teleological argument. I enjoy recounting a story told by the English apologist J. Edwin Orr. It seems that he was walking along the sea-shore, and came across sand scooped out in the shape of our continents. Now, he could have imagined that this was done by some enterprising crab, but thought it the work of a more intelligent being. As he continued along the beach, his impression was validated; for there he came across a little girl with shovel and bucket in hand. She had been demonstrating her grasp of world geography.

Immanuel Kant considered this argument from design the oldest, clearest, and most common sense argument ever devised. Conversely, one would expect order and adaptation within bounded systems. Then, too, the analogy may be weak. In any case, the results (as with the previous argument) fall considerably short of God as revealed in Holy Writ.

We will allow the scientist/theologian John Polkinghorne to pick up the discussion at this juncture. With reference to the efficient optical

system of the human eye, he inquires:

> Didn't such signs of design point one inevitably to the presence of a
> Designer? It all sounded pretty convincing, until Darwin drew the rug
> from beneath such author's feet by showing how his theory of evolution
> could account for apparent design *without* the intervention of a divine
> Designer.[11]

Interrogating himself further, Polkinghorne asks: "So am I going to
make the same mistake all over again? I think not." With this, he alludes
to the *God of the gaps* as a means of managing the inexplicable. "If God's
the Creator," he concludes, "he's somehow connected with the whole
show, not just the difficult or murky bits of what's going on."

With such in mind, ought we to conjecture beyond where science can
confidently guide us? Polkinghorne does not hesitate in answering to the
affirmative, since science raises questions it cannot itself answer. In
particular, why can we do science in the first place, and why is the
universe so special? Some pages later, he sums up this line of reasoning:

> In actual fact, I don't think one can *prove* that God exists or that he doesn't
> exist--we're in an area of discussion that is too deep for mere proof. I *am*
> saying that the existence of the Creator would explain why the world is so
> profoundly intelligible, and I can't see any other explanation that works
> half as well.[12]

Chaos theory might, as a result, be said to refine the traditional
argument so as to assure its comprehensive character. It decidedly does
not eliminate it as a legitimate consideration among others. We cannot in
any case be satisfied with less than making sense out of life, and investing
it with personal meaning.

Moral argument.

> In his *Critique of Pure Reason*, Kant represented speculative reason
> capable of organizing sense experience but not dealing with divine reality.
> In his *Critique of Practical Reason*, he pointed out that the sense of moral
> obligation required that we postulate the existence of God, freedom, and
> immortality.[13]

In its simplest form, he argues in a cause-effect manner from the sense of
ought to a source for moral order--associated with God.

A more subtle form of the argument suggests that in recognizing a
moral dimension of life we implicitly assume a transcendent source,

whether in fact we identify it as *God* or not. If by any other name, we still invoke the Almighty.

The naturalist will insist, perhaps unconvincingly, that moral codes simply evolve to meet human needs. As such, they may be thought of as survival techniques. Moreover, as with the other arguments, the results fall short of that testified to by the prophets and Jesus.

As for chaos theory, it seems to ease into moral considerations with its characteristic accent on life as open to creative possibilities. Paul Davies comments as follows: "Some people have seized on the openness to argue for the reality of human free will. Others claim that it bestows upon nature an element of creativity, and ability to bring forth that which is genuinely new."[14] In any case, he concludes that the final chapter has yet to be written.

If so, what obligation should we feel in this regard? Why this and not that? Who makes the final determination? Such disturbing questions would seem to assure us that the moral argument will not only remain current, but likely take on new urgency.

Ontological argument. Anselm's ontological argument seems to me the most tantalizing of the theistic alternatives. Often written off, it comes back with renewed vigor.

> Anselm reasoned that God is a being than which nothing greater exists. Strictly speaking, his argument is valid only insofar as the human perception can be identified with God. Nonetheless, the widespread and persisting character of religious experience cannot be taken lightly.[15]

At some point, it would seem more likely that God exists than not.

Increasingly, it appears that chaos theorists promote intuition coupled with scientific precision. This brings to mind a classic comment by Blaise Pascal: "But in the intuitive mind the principles are found in common use, and are before the eyes of everybody. One has only to look and no effort is necessary; it is only a question of good eyesight."[16]

The fact is that we cannot decide beforehand the nature of reality.

> This can only be discovered by submitting ourselves to actual experience. So, you see, it's not a case of scientific fact versus religious opinion. It's a case, with both science and religion, of trying to interpret and understand the rich, varied, and surprising way the would actually is.[17]

Biblical faith has as a rule nurtured scientific investigation. First, with accent on the world as God's creation, and for that reason of critical importance. Second, with emphasis on the viability of doing so, inasmuch as creation reflects a divinely sanctioned order. Third, without impunity, since creation is distinct from its Creator. Some chaos theorists often appear inclined to begin repaying this indebtedness. It remains to be seen how seriously they will take this obligation.

C. Stephen Evans appropriately concludes: "Whether the arguments are rationally convincing to someone depends in each case on accepting some key premise or premises which are neither self-evident nor absolutely certain."[18] He nonetheless adds: "It would seem that such arguments, individually and collectively, could form a case for the reasonableness of theism, at least relative to its rivals." Most of all as compared with its rivals. Given a broader understanding of the arguments, associated with a comprehensive sense of life and personal involvement, chaos theory would appear sympathetic.

The Experience of Pain

Years ago and in another context, I wrote: "We generally treat the Book of Job as a commentary on suffering, but it is much more than that. *Pain* certainly rushes to the forefront (both as physical affliction and mental anguish), but *wisdom* is the more persisting subject."[19] A hundred pages later, I concluded my observations on how we can handle suffering constructively. Here we simply sketch the line of reasoning before touching on chaos theory.

First, it is critical to recognize life in general and suffering in particular within God's benevolent design. It is not for lack of divine compassion, but our intractability that we do not fare better. C.S. Lewis presses this persuasion to conclude that a loving God reluctantly provides hell for those who will embrace nothing better from Him.

We live from the *middle*, between the garden and glory. Here, again to borrow from Lewis, we experience *complex good*, i.e., good filtered through a fallen world desperately in need of redemption. If we cultivate such good as we experience, we will live a fuller life; if not, we will have wasted an inviting opportunity.

Second, we must cultivate piety throughout a wide range of experiences, some good and some bad. Augustine had the latter in mind when he observed that both the wicked and godly suffer, but where the former become bitter and callous, the latter hopefully become resolute in their faith. It is our *response* to pain that makes the dramatic difference.

In so doing, we point beyond changing circumstances to what remains constant. In particular, as regards God's faithfulness, our obligation, and a realistic potential.

Third, welcome ambiguity as an intricate aspect of life. Eliphaz, one of Job's aggravating associates, conversely reduced life to the simplistic formula that the good prosper and the evil suffer.

"Relent," Job cautions in response, "do not be unjust; reconsider, for my integrity is at stake" (6:29). With this, he insists that matters can be variously interpreted. Not only that, but he supposes that he has a better grasp on reality than his accuser. Thirty-six chapters later, God validates his opinion.

Fourth, learn from tradition without being enslaved to it. Bildad replaces Eliphaz as Job's interrogator. "Ask the former generations and find out what their fathers learned, for we were born only yesterday and know nothing, and the days on earth are but a shadow" (8:8). While not without merit, Bildad's advice given the circumstances appears as trite and even cruel.

Job has by this time moved well beyond any unqualified appeal to the past. On the one hand, he does not intend to neglect tradition; on the other, he does not concede that it can pass for the present. As a result, he will manage as best he can in anticipation of the future as in God's providence.

Fifth, root out prejudice.

> Zophar brashly announced that God had exacted less from Job than his guilt deserved (11:6) and followed up this presumptive charge with a clear distortion of the patriarch's behavior (20:18-21). His prejudice (reaching a decision before weighing the evidence) drips with each succeeding comment.[20]

Whereupon, Job replies: "Listen carefully to my words, let this be the consolation you give me" (21:1). After this, he sets out to deliberately weigh the evidence. In conclusion, he sets aside the charge brought against him: "So how can you console me with your nonsense? Nothing is left of your answers but falsehood!" (21:34).

Sixth, cultivate faith in contrast to credulity. Two concerns encouraged Elihu to break his self-imposed silence: Job's insistence that he was innocent, and his associates' inability to convince him otherwise. "Wait for me," he urged Job, "and I will show you there is yet more to be said in God's behalf" (36:2).

The issue of credibility heightens with Elihu.

> No one should doubt the necessity of having faith. To negotiate life at all,

we must believe in something, somehow. We cannot choose whether to believe, but we must decide among the vast array of possibilities presented for our consideration. Here Job finds himself, as must we all.[21]

Seventh, posture with reference to God. We live in His world, by His grace, to do His bidding. This is the only way life ultimately makes sense.

We ought consequently not to aim too high or too low. That is to say, we were not created as gods, nor simply as brute beasts. We were given a privileged place as stewards of God's extended creation. We will have to give account for how well we have assumed our obligation.

Finally, posture with reference to others. As one *with* others, we are objects of God's concern. As one *for* others, we are meant to serve His benevolent purposes. As one *among* others, we are to benefit from their ministry voluntarily rendered.

"After Job had prayed for his friends, the Lord made him prosperous again and gave him twice as much as he had before" (42:1). Such was the happy ending to an otherwise tragic narrative. Wisdom triumphed in the end.

How might a person of faith couple all this with a chaos orientation? John Polkinghorne serves as a prime case in point:

> The world in which we actually live is multi-layered in the richness of its reality. ...Our scientific explorations are insights into the rational order with which God has endowed his universe. Our experiences of beauty are a sharing in his joy in creation. Our moral perceptions are intuitions of his good and perfect will. Our religious experiences are encounters with his hidden presence. Such a view is whole and satisfying. It has the ring of truth about it. Who are we? We are God's creatures.[22]

As for suffering, it must be expected in a world torn by spiritual conflict. Even so, it can serve the greater good. As Paul confidently exclaims: "And we know that in all things God works for the good of those who love him, who have been called according to his purpose" (Rom. 8:28).

Prospects of a Paradigm Shift

According to Thomas Kuhn's thesis in his influential *The Structure of Scientific Revolutions* (1962), scientists like the rest of humanity

> carry out their day-to-day affairs within a framework of presuppositions about what constitutes a problem, a solution, and a method. Such a background of shared assumptions makes up a paradigm, and at any given

time a particular scientific community will have a prevailing paradigm that shapes and directs work in the field.[23]

From time to time, the prevailing paradigm shifts to accommodate new data, account for deficiencies in the previous paradigm, and provide opportunity for further investigation. Such a *shift* would seem to be in progress with regard to the chaos paradigm. Heinz-Otto Peitgen comments:

> For many, chaos theory already belongs among the greatest achievements in the natural sciences in this century. Indeed, it can be claimed that very few developments in the natural sciences have awakened so much public interest. Here and there, we even hear of changing images of reality or of a revolution in the natural sciences.[24]

If so, we can expect strong opposition, especially from invested interests. As with any other revolution, blood may flow--figuratively speaking. We are reluctant to surrender our paradigms, since we have invested them with virtually religious character.

If so, we may also expect support from unlikely places. Those most instrumental in paradigm shifts have often been the younger or less experienced scholars, with less to lose. These moreover form unexpected alliances to further a common cause.

If so, the shift may likewise come in a painfully slow manner. It takes time to set aside former ways of viewing reality, and thinking through the implications of an alternative. In addition, the more comprehensive a shift, other things being equal, the longer it takes, and it is difficult to imagine a more comprehensive paradigm than chaos--apart from introducing a religious or philosophical dimension.

In particular, the evolutionary paradigm in at least its extended application seems threatened. In natural science, *evolution* refers to the gradual and continuous process by which the first and most primitive of living organisms was thought to be developed into the diversity of plant and animal life as we know it today. As applied to a wide range of disciplines, *evolutionary theory* implies the gradual emergence from primitive ways of thinking to more mature alternatives.

As for natural science, Russell Mixter writes:

> If the trend of the time continues, new fossils will be found. However, until a major group of organisms such as an order, is connected to another order by a closely graded series of forms, one need not hold to the interpretation which derives the members of an order from some other

order.[25]

As if to illustrate his point, Mixter adds that one might assume *the ancestral types of the group* are specifically created rather than descended from some antecedent. That is to say, either might be correct. Otherwise expressed, he calls into question what some deride as *the myth of scientific objectivity*.

As for a broader application, the evolutionary paradigm becomes considerably less persuasive. William Roweton consequently complains that many assume that *the human psychological process* is best studied on the basis of animal behavior. "This approach," he concludes, "distorts and fragments many characteristic human traits; and, while educational researchers have been besieged with intricate child rearing and instructional questions, success in finding the answers has been qualified."[26]

Conversely, according to Roweton, human learning and development "are dynamic, irregular, individualistic, seemingly unpredictable, and distinctively unique in nature." Which, if true, would welcome a paradigm shift to accommodate their manifestly chaotic character.

Given the above line of reasoning, several conclusions can be readily drawn. First, the prevailing evolutionary paradigm enjoys wide acceptance. This brings to mind the public school policy concerning the teaching of evolution: "Schools may teach about explanations of life on earth, including religious ones, in comparative religion or social studies classes. In science classes, however, they may present only genuinely scientific critiques of any explanation of life on earth."[27]

Second, evolution as a prevailing paradigm is subject to serious limitations. We documented this first in connection with natural science, and thereafter with behavioral science. It is as we sense inadequacy with a current paradigm that we look around for a likely replacement.

Third, conventional wisdom assumes that only the evolutionary paradigm meets scientific criteria. While this may be to confuse the scientific method with naturalistic presuppositions, the chaos paradigm arises from natural science to rival a questionable assumption.

Fourth, the chaos paradigm proposes not to follow in the reductionism of its predecessor. "Chaos is antireductionistic," James Gleick insists.

> This new science makes a strong claim about the world, namely, that when it comes to the most interesting questions, questions about order and disorder, decay and creativity, pattern formation and life itself, the whole cannot be explained in terms of the parts.[28]

Fifth, the chaos paradigm invites religious dialogue as a means of further exploring reality. Richard Feynman's comment is illustrative:

> The great era of awakening of human intellect may well produce a method of understanding the qualitative content of equations. ...We cannot say whether something beyond it, like God is needed or not. And so we can all hold strong opinions either way.[29]

Sixth, whatever success we enjoy in pursuit of better understanding, we can be assured that as the heavens are higher than the earth, so are God's ways than ours (cf. Isa. 55:9). This realization likely solicits John Polkinghorne's cogent observation: "God's action within the cloudiness of unpredictable open process will always be hidden; it cannot be demonstrated by experiment, though it may be discerned by faith."[30]

Seventh, the chaos paradigm offers to level the playing field for those of religious faith in general, and the Christian faith in particular. As mentioned earlier, science raises questions in chaos perspective that it cannot in and of itself answer. We have reason to hope that chaos theory will foster less competition between science and faith commitment, and more cooperation.

Editorial note. The above ought especially to be compared with *My Servant Job* (1979)--as a fuller treatment of the enigmatic character of suffering; and *A Case For Christianity* (1997)--as a more comprehensive apologetic endeavor. Its apologetic interest is shared with an earlier article: *The Apologetic Use of Sign in the Fourth Gospel,* and its chaos orientation with the remaining entry: *Chaos and the Moral Imperative.*

ENDNOTES

1. James Gleick, *Chaos: The Software*, p. 4.
2. Ian Percival, "Chaos: A Science for the Real World," *Exploring Chaos* (Hall, ed.), p. 11.
3. Ibid., p. 15.
4. Peter Coveney, "Chaos, Entrophy, and the Arrow of Time," *Exploring Chaos* (Hall, ed.), p. 203.
5. Ibid., p. 212.
6. John Casti, *Paradigms Lost*, p. 11.
7. Jacob Licht, *Storytelling in the Bible*, p. 9.
8. William Barclay, *Jesus as They Saw Him*, p. 15.
9. Morris Inch, *A Case For Christianity*, pp. 49-50.
10. Casti, *op. cit.*, p. 494.
11. John Polkinghorne, *Quarks, Chaos, and Christianity*, p. 21.
12. Ibid., p. 25.
13. Inch, *op. cit.*, p. 51.
14. Paul Davies, "Is the Universe a Machine?" *Exploring Chaos* (Hall, ed.), p. 221.
15. Inch, *op. cit.*, p. 52.
16. Blaise Pascal, *Pensees*, p. 75.
17. Polkinghorne, *op. cit.*, p. 17.
18. C. Stephen Evans, *Philosophy of Religion*, p. 75.
19. Morris Inch, *My Servant Job*, p. 9.
20. Ibid., p. 64.
21. Ibid., p. 76.
22. Polkinghorne, *op. cit.*, p. 61.
23. Casti, *op. cit.*, p. 40.
24. Hans-Otto Peitgen, "The Causality Principle, Deterministic Laws and Chaos," *Chaos: The New Science* (Holte, ed.), p. 35.
25. Russell Mixter, "Creation and Evolution," *Creationism in the 20th-Century America* (Numbers, ed.), Vol. 10, p. 209.
26. William Roweton (ed.), *Revitalizing Educational Psychology*, p. 1.
27. *Religion in the Public Schools: A Joint Statement of Current Law*, p. 3.
28. James Gleick, "Chaos and Beyond," *Chaos: The New Science* (Holte, ed.), p. 125.

29. Ibid., p. 127.
30. John Polkinghorne, "Chaos and Cosmos: A Theological Approach," *Chaos: The New Science* (Holte, ed.), p.115.

BIBLIOGRAPHY

Barclay, William. *Jesus as They Saw Him.* New York: Harper & Row, 1962.

Casti, John. *Paradigms Lost: Images of Man in the Mirror of Science.* New York: Morrow, 1989.

Coveney, Peter. "Chaos, Entrophy, and the Arrow of Time," *Exploring Chaos* (Hall, ed.), 203-212.

Davies, Paul. "Is the Universe a Machine?" *Exploring Chaos* (Hall, ed.), 213-221.

Evans, C. Stephen. *Philosophy of Religion: Thinking About Faith.* Downers Grove: InterVarsity, 1982.

Gleick, James. "Chaos and Beyond," *Chaos: The New Science* (Holte, ed.), 119-127.

_____. *Chaos: The Software.* Scotts Valley: Autodesk, 1991.

Hall, Nina (ed.). *Exploring Chaos.* New York: Norton, 1991.

Holte, John (ed.) *Chaos: The New Science.* Lanham: University Press of America, 1993.

Inch, Morris. *A Case For Christianity.* Wheaton: Tyndale House, 1997.

_____. *My Servant Job.* Grand Rapids: Baker, 1979.

Licht, Jacob. *Storytelling in the Bible.* Jerusalem: Magnes, 1986.

Mixter, Russell. "Creation and Evolution," *Creationism in 20th-Century America* (Numbers, ed.), Vol. 10, 185-217.

Numbers, Ronald (ed.). *Creationism in 20th-Century America*, 10 vols. New York: Garland, 1995.

Pascal, Blaise. *Pensees.* Baltimore: Penguin, 1995.

Percival, Ian. "Chaos: A Science for the Real World," *Exploring Chaos* (Hall, ed.), 11-21.

Peitgen, Heinz-Otto. "The Causality Principle, Deterministic Laws and Chaos," *Chaos: The New Science* (Holte, ed.), 35-43.

Polkinghorne, John. "Chaos and Cosmos: A Theological Approach," *Chaos: The New Science* (Holte, ed.), 105-117.

_____, *Quarks, Chaos and Christianity: Questions to Science and Religion.* New York: Crossroad, 1997.

Religion in the Public Schools: A Joint Statement of Current Law. New York: Religion in the Public Schools, 1995.

CHAOS AND THE MORAL IMPERATIVE

"It has a great name," S. Neil Rasband comments.

It generates pretty pictures. It represents the very latest thing in science. It is relatively accessible. But besides these trappings, it must be admitted that chaos theory challenges many of our presuppositions, and makes us think differently about our world.[1]

It is in this last connection that we invoke chaos theory as a means to recast our understanding of Christian ethics.

Daniel Kaplan and Leon Glass define chaos as "aperiodic bounded dynamics in a deterministic system with sensitive dependence on initial conditions."[2] *Aperiodic* means that no state is simply repeated. *Bounded* suggests that these successive states occur within a finite range. *Deterministic* signifies that what transpires is conditioned. *Sensitive dependence* points back toward a common origin for subsequent developments. As observed in chaos theory, order gives way to chaos and chaos to order.

As for Christian ethics, we take this to mean the obligation that Christian faith puts on how we behave. This involves our relationship to God and others, our personal development, and the way we manage our natural resources. It purposes to help us live in God's world, by His grace, and for His glory.

Jeremiah's Vision

Jeremiah revealed his personal feelings as no other of the Hebrew prophets. He had no desire to play the prophet of doom, but felt constrained to warn his people of impending destruction. Whereupon, he "looked at the earth, and it was formless and empty, and at the heavens, and their light was gone" (4:23). He "looked at the mountains, and they were quaking; all the hills were swaying." He "looked, and there were not people; every bird in the sky had flown away." He "looked, and the fruitful land was a desert; all its towns lay in ruins before the Lord, before his fierce anger."

The prophet instinctively thinks of the primeval chaos (Gen. 2:1), before God brought order and declared it good. Now chaos had returned at the invitation of a rebellious people and as an expression of God's wrath. Herewith, we are introduced to chaos reality in religious and moral perspective.

We are moreover reminded of our *sensitive dependence* on original conditions. As Derek Kidner observes, "if God alone brings form out of formlessness, He alone sustains it."[3] One cannot hope to get along in God's world without God. The more things change, the more similar they appear.

"Righteousness exalts a nation, but sin is a disgrace to any people" (Prov. 14:34). No exception is made, and none intended. Judah was not an exception to the rule, but a case in point.

"On the basis of the various explanations put forward for the emergence of life here on Earth," John Casti reflects, "my impression is that should the Earth be wiped clean of all life today in some kind of planetary Armageddon, the likelihood of life forms of any kind reemerging in a few billion years would be a bet that not even Lloyd's of London would put on the board."[4] With this, he further concludes that there is something special not only about humans, but life in general. This would have come as no surprise to the prophet, who attributed this *something special* to God's creative design and providential implementation.

Three constants are suggested by the Biblical narrative. First, we encounter man's characteristic waywardness. Given a choice, we all too often make the wrong one. Having done so, we persist. Should we come to our senses, it is often too late to escape the dire consequences.

Second, we discover God's faithfulness. While distressed with the behavior of His prodigal people, He has not given up on them. As someone has observed, it is better to be in the hands of an angry God than to fall out of them.

Third, God invites others to further His redemptive interests. If Jeremiah was a special person for a particular occasion, so are we. If he felt himself insufficient for his ministry, so might we. If God's grace was adequate for him, so for us.

All things considered, we have observed an *openness* with Jeremiah's vision, as with life in general.

> Some people have seized on this openness to argue for the reality of free will. Others claim that it bestows on creation an element of creativity.... . Whatever the merits of such sweeping claims, it seems safe to conclude from the study of chaos that the future of the Universe is not irredeemably fixed.[5]

Qualifications aside, the final chapter has still to be written.

Up to this point, we have approached the topic in a concrete historical setting. Henceforth, we will lift out several Biblical motifs for discussion. While these provide valuable building blocks, they fall considerably short of a comprehensive treatment of the topic.

Evolving Motifs

Oughtness motif. "To think contemplatively is to ask oneself what *is*; to think operatively is to ask oneself what to *do*."[6]   The latter must be guided, limited, and qualified by the former. Otherwise stated, what one is obligated to do falls within what can be done, and does not extend to what is impossible to do. Moral responsibility occurs within finite boundaries.

Even so, what we perceive as parameters may be self-imposed. God had greater things for Jeremiah than he could have imagined. As is often the case, we need to gain higher ground in order to employ our genuine potential. Accordingly, we are encouraged not to ask for tasks commensurate to our abilities, but abilities commensurate to our tasks.

C.G. Montefiore reflects from a Jewish perspective on the distinctive dynamic of Jesus' appeal: "Jesus seems...to have perceived the good lurking under the evil. He could quench the evil and quicken the good by giving to the sinner somebody to admire and love. He asked for service, and put it in the place of sin."[7]   While much more could be added, this calls our attention to the moral dynamic at work, and primes us for what follows.

The situation is decidedly more complicated than it might first appear, and as Montefiore subsequently allows. For one thing, we are in large measure the product of socialization. "*Socialization* is a learning process through which people acquire the beliefs, values, and social behavior characteristics of their culture or subculture largely through social modeling and instruction."[8]   Since in chaos theory complex systems are extremely sensitive to initial conditions, even a small variation early on will be greatly amplified with the passing of time.

Consider a case in point. Certain Pharisees came to Jesus with the question: "Is it lawful for a man to divorce his wife?" (Mark 10:2). Jesus cuts across their casuistry with an appeal to the Law: "What did Moses command you?" "Moses permitted a man to write a certificate of divorce and send her away," they replied. Jesus observed that this was because of their hardness of heart, and not the original intent. He thereby directed their attention back to the original intent before it was obscured by subsequent rationalizations.

Whereas Jesus' appeal was calculated to get the issue back on track, it did not address specifics. "To behave appropriately in a changing and/or complex world, one cannot always do the same thing. Flexibility is required for dealing with the issues and problems encountered in life."[9] With such in view, Jesus complained about those who "tie up heavy loads and put them on men's shoulders, but they themselves are not willing to lift a finger to move them" (Matt. 23:4).

This brings us to weigh the role of *moral judgments*. They are said to involve (1) the examination and clarification of choices, (2) an elaboration of consequences, (3) imaginative identification with those most implicated, (4) evaluation and comparison of the values involved, and (5) decision. The process requires logic tempered by intuition. To add the obvious, it is also fallible.

On the other hand, God delights in using human means to achieve divine ends. Thus while He punishes evil to the third and fourth generation, He rewards good to a thousand generations (Exod. 20:6). As noted from time to time in chaos theory, "if God rolled dice, He would win." Seemingly more to the point, if He rolled dice, they would be loaded.

In a manner of speaking, there are two moralities: one that conforms to convention and the other that allows for revelation. Christians are obligated to the former insofar as it contributes to social order and does not conflict with faith, and the latter as it transcends common morality. Whereas we render to Caesar the things of Caesar, and to God the things of God, God's concerns take priority.

Jeremiah appealed for his contemporaries to repent of their sins and be reconciled to God. It was certainly not the best of times. The past was catching up with them. They were slow to respond. Disaster appeared imminent.

Conversely, it was not the worst of times. God was still encouraging them to mend their ways. They could make the best of a bad situation.

If carried off into captivity, they might be restored. While in a far country, they could be consoled.

One thing more,

> The task that God has assigned his people is not only to heed the word of the Lord but also to wait for this word. It is not only to assess the implications of his commandment but also to prepare ourselves to hear it in the light that comes to us from Holy Scripture.[10]

We thereby come to distinguish His voice from the babble of sounds around us.

Reflection motif. "So God created man in his own image, in the image of God he created him; male and female he created them" (Gen. 1:27). The term *likeness* is dropped from the earlier deliberation (v. 26), suggesting that it and *image* were meant to reenforce one another. Such fine distinctions as may exist do not justify the ponderous theological discussion allotted to them.

Man *in his totality* was made in God's image. Scripture does not explicitly distinguish between his spiritual and corporeal character in this connection, however we may eventually account for it. It moreover extends the image to include woman.

Man was *uniquely* created in God's image. We are initially alerted to this fact by the divine counsel. This is confirmed by subsequent developments.

He consequently could communicate and have fellowship with his Creator. Sin would bring alienation, and with it the need for reconciliation.

God subsequently placed man in the Garden of Eden, and instructed him: "You are free to eat from any tree in the garden; but you must not eat from the tree of the knowledge of good and evil, for when you eat of it you will surely die" (2:16-17). Walter Brueggemann comments: "Human beings before God are characterized by *vocation, permission,* and *prohibition.* The God of the garden is chiefly remembered as the one who prohibits. But the prohibition makes sense only in terms of the other two."[11]

As for *vocation,* man was made steward of God's creation. God thereupon brought the animals for Adam to name (2:19-20), suggesting his dominion over them. In naming them, he exercises the gift of language, and an obligation in keeping with his unique capacities.

As for *permission,* God's provision is exceedingly generous. Even so, Jewish commentators are quick to point out that the provision presupposes man's compliance with stewardship obligations. In other words, work first and partake later.

As for *prohibition, good and evil* appear idiomatic for *comprehensiveness* (cf. 24:50; 31:24, 29). Thus to eat from the forbidden fruit was to assume autonomy. God was no longer welcome.

Man's defection involved two elements. First, it expressed a lack of trust. "You will not surely die," the serpent encouraged Eve. "Or God knows that when you eat of it your eyes will be opened, and you will be like God, knowing good and evil" (3:4). It was the serpent's word against God's, and the former seemed more convincing.

Second, it assumed an adversarial relationship. "To be *as God*, and to achieve it by outwitting Him, is an intoxicating programme. God will henceforth be regarded, consciously or not, as rival and enemy."[12]

Mankind bore a lingering reminder of his defection. There would be continued enmity between the seed and that of the serpent. The earth would no longer readily cooperate, but only as a result of burdensome toil. The woman would travail in giving birth.

While the way ahead appeared difficult, it was not impossible. God had not absented Himself. There was even a veiled promise concerning eventual triumph of the woman's seed (Gen. 3:15). Jesus' characteristic preference for God as *Father*, with its corollary *son*, suggests that the former may still be reflected in the latter.

All things considered, Robert Seltzer cogently concludes:

> We have a series of tales in which the world, created by God to be good and containing one creature in God's image, turned out full of violent, murderous, and self-glorifying men. This state of affairs, in turn, leads to the formation of people nurtured by God capable of producing a few individuals of satisfactory spiritual nature, but in the main those who are obtuse, unfaithful, and frequently backsliding from the divinely given task.[11]

Given a *sensitive dependence on initial conditions*, the results were not surprising.

Likewise from chaos perspective, man's defection might be said to violate the conditions of *non-linearity*. That is, it rejected the complex network of relationships characterizing creation at its inception. In theory and practice, this could be done either in aspiring to be *as God* or in settling for less than God meant man to be. Otherwise stated, either by *deification* or *reductionism*.

"Yet at present we do not see everything subject to man," the author of Hebrews observes. "But we see Jesus, who was made a little lower than the angels, now crowned with glory and honor because he suffered death, so that by the grace of God he might taste death for everyone" (2:8-9).

As a result, Paul encourages his readers "to put on the new self, created to be like God in true righteousness and holiness" (Eph. 4:24). He likewise exhorts them: "Do not lie to each other, since you have taken off your old self with its practices and have put on the new self, which is being renewed in knowledge in the image of its Creator" (Col. 3:9-10). The apostle's *good news* "is that now, in Christ, God is at work restoring that lost image. This restoration or re-creation is not mankind's work at all; it is not a process of giving up some vices and accepting a few virtues. This *new self* is God's doing."[14]

This brings us to conclude that Christian ethics, qualifications notwithstanding, amounts to *theonomous ethics.* They are God-generated, God-activated, and God-implemented. Man can cooperate but not initiate.

Creative motif. While this theme could readily be considered in the above context, it seems best to single it out for special attention. Man resembles God in his capacity to create.

The creation account reveals considerable similarities with other High God traditions. Not uncommonly, God appears as a celestial potter. First, He casts the clay. It is at this juncture formless. Next, He begins to fashion a vessel. If successful, He will comment appreciatively on the finished work.

If not, He will recast the clay and begin over. Sometimes this results in a modified design. In any case, no project proves too difficult for Him to manage.

The pattern is unmistakable. It begins with imagination, proceeds through a chaotic phase, and concludes with order. When necessary, the latter stages are repeated to gain the proper results.

"The Pentateuch begins with a description of God as creator of heaven and earth (Gen. 11:1), and it ends with a reference to God as the Father and Creator of Israel (Deut. 32:6, 15)."[15] The term for *create (bara)* occurs five times in Genesis 1, and another five times between Genesis 2:4 and 6:7. God is the subject, and no reference is made to pre-existing material. That is, chaos would appear as if an interim stage in the creative process.

God's creative disposition carries over from the natural world into history. "Go down to the potter's house," God instructs Jeremiah, "and I will give you my message" (Jer. 18:2).   So he did as directed. Whereupon, he observed the potter at work. "But the pot he was shaping from the clay was marred in his hands, so the potter formed it into another pot, shaping it as seemed best to him." Then the word of God came to the prophet: "O house of Israel, can I not do with you as this potter does? Like clay in the hand of the potter, so are you in my hand, O house of Israel."

Man seeks to emulate God in various ways, not least of which is his bent toward creativity.   That is, we attempt to construct something original, or modify in some novel manner what already exists.

While much has been written on the subject of creativity, we will limit our discussion to three considerations that seem especially relevant for our current topic.   First, so as to bring order out of perceived chaos. Jacques Maquet elaborates: "Our individual and collective security is constantly imperiled by entropy.   At a deep level of the mind, we fear chaos and strive to control it by maintaining or establishing order."[16]

Conservative and creative approaches contrast in Jesus' response to the disciples of John concerning fasting (Matt. 9:14-17).   Herewith, Jesus suggests that so long as He is with them, they ought to rejoice.   Fasting would be appropriate at a later time.   Hereafter, Jesus adds two illustrations to emphasize the discontinuity between the old forms of worship and a new spirit of creativity.

> No one sews a patch of unshrunk cloth on an old garment, for the patch will pull away from the garment, making the tear worse.   Neither do men pour new wine into old wineskins.   If they do, the skins will burst, the wine will run out and the wineskins will be ruined.

If, however, they creatively pour new wine into new wineskins, both will be preserved.

Second, so as to convey a transcendent reality.

> This abhorrence of disorder is transposed, at a philosophical level, into systems of thought which attempt to comprehend the eternal world-- comprehend in the sense of intellectually understand, as well as in the sense of comprise and embrace.[17]

In this connection, we can better appreciate Jesus' preaching *the good news of the kingdom* (Matt. 4:23). Jesus announced the arrival of the long anticipated time of God's deliverance.   The miracles that attended His preaching were as if an earnest of what was yet to come.   These taken together resembled a window opened into heaven.

Third, so as to please God.

> If a painter, intoxicated with other wine than that of our vineyards, *paints only to please God*, he can be a good or a bad painter, and he does not become a better painter by the very fact, but he is put in a position to use his virtue of art in the purest and freest manner.[18]

So it was when the apostles were charged no longer to mention the name of Jesus, Peter and John replied: "Judge for yourselves whether it is right in God's sight to obey you rather than God. For we cannot help speaking about what we have seen and heard" (Acts 4:19-20). In being faithful to their calling, they supposed themselves a creative vanguard of God's latter day contingent.

Disciple motif. The *disciple* is a student. His/her course of study involves not only the quest of knowledge but the appropriation of wisdom. This, in turn, introduces him/her into the actual world. Here we experience chaos reality.

Here also we encounter Jesus. He not only taught but exemplified the way of righteousness. In the latter connection, He models kingdom ethics.

We will draw on a previous study concerning Jesus' exhortations to steer us through the present discussion. These relate to the Messiah, the Kingdom of Heaven (God), the Scriptures, the community, its mission, and the consummation. As for the Messiah, "Given time and ingenuity, the rabbis would identify no less than 456 Biblical references to the Deliverer. One could easily imagine devout Jews pouring over the sacred text to add to a growing Messianic legacy."[19]

Three words characterize Jesus' Messianic appeal as none others: "Come, follow me." By way of example, He employed this poignant formula when calling Peter and Andrew (Matt. 4:19), in response to the would-be disciple who asked first to bury his parents (8:22), in calling Matthew (9:9), and after admonishing a young man to sell all that he had and give to the needy (19:21).

In following Jesus, they were to manage chaos constructively. When their boat threatened to capsize, trust. When called upon to feed a famished multitude, act. When facing persecution, pray. When facing death, believe. As a word of encouragement, "There is no place, no experience of life in this or any world, which is beyond the reach of the love of God as we know it in Jesus Christ."[20]

Jesus came preaching: "Repent, for the kingdom of heaven is near"

(Matt. 4:17). Differences aside, there was sufficient in common between Jesus' understanding and that of His contemporaries to provide a point of contact. The latter nonetheless thought largely in political terms. Jesus conversely emphasized God's reign in perpetuity, with the inauguration of His advent, and with future consummation.

John Casti suggests three models for understanding the relationship between science and religion: as two distinct realms, as in agreement, and as partial expressions of the same ultimate reality. His preference can be seen in the observation that "a theology that attaches itself to one scientific family today will surely be an orphan tomorrow."[21] His logic suits Friedrich Gogarten, who advised that we face life with reciprocal care for one another, while open to the mystery of God's working with us. Such is in brief what we can make out of Jesus' kingdom accent in chaos perspective.

"It is written" was Jesus' favorite way of alluding to Scripture. He employed it three times when tempted (Matt. 4:4, 7, 10), again when cleansing the temple (21:13), and still again to account for the disciples falling away (26:31). Neither time nor circumstances would alter the conditions. "I tell you the truth, until heaven and earth disappear, not the smallest letter, not the least stroke of the pen, will by any means disappear from the Law until everything is accomplished" (5:18).

In this connection, it is worth noting that Scripture does not categorically stigmatize chaos. The latter first appears as an interim stage in creation, and subsequently as a step in creative enterprise. It also appears as a wilderness access to the promised land.

Those who came to Jesus found themselves in community. "The disciples did not learn of fellowship in the abstract, but as they jostled about following Jesus. ...Each day and each event contributed to their understanding and appreciation of life in Christ and as community."[22]

"If your brother sins against you, go and show him his fault," Jesus advised (Matt. 18:18). If he listens, you have won him over. If not, involve others. If previous efforts fail, bring it before the congregation. Do what you can to keep chaos from encroaching on community. As a final resort, remove the disruptive offender. In this and other ways, learn how to manage chaos in and through life together.

Jesus urged those who came in faith to go in service. Having announced that all power was delegated to Him, Jesus mandated "go and make disciples of all nations, baptizing them in the name of the Father and of the Son and of the Holy Spirit, and teaching them to observe everything I have commanded you" (Matt. 28:19-20). With this, Jesus assured the disciples that He would be with them always, even to the end of the age.

Such would imply a constant purpose realized in complex and unpredictable situations. In chaos jargon:

> Although broad patterns in the rise and fall of civilizations may be sketched, events never repeat exactly--history is aperiodic. And history books teem with examples of small events that led to momentous and long-lasting changes in the course of human affairs.[23]

As Jesus was walking away from the temple, the disciples called attention to its lavish construction. Whereupon, Jesus responded: "I tell you a truth, not one stone here will be left on another; every one will be thrown down" (Matt. 24:2). "When will this happen," they inquired, "and what will be the sign of your coming and of the end of the age?" "Jesus tailored His response to distinguish between the two. While Jerusalem's days were numbered, His return remained indefinite, following a time of severe tribulation."[24]

The disciples were not to live in the past, or become enamored of the relics of past accomplishment. They were to live toward the future. In this, they resembled a people before their time

All things considered, the disciple assumed a pilgrimage from the city of destruction to that of everlasting bliss. Former things were passing away; all things were becoming new. Hope in chaos perspective springs eternal.

Neighbor motif. Once Jesus told what was perhaps a true story, concerning an injured man and those who observed his plight (Luke 10:29-37). Its setting was the Jericho Road, winding its way nearly seventeen miles from Jericho to Jerusalem, and rising about thirteen hundred feet in the process. Jerome described it as still being infested with robbers by the late fourth century.

It seems that the man fell prey to brigands, who left him half dead by the wayside. There he would perish unless someone came to his aid. After an indeterminate time, a priest came by. Surveying the situation, he scurried by on the far side of the road. Subsequently, a Levite came along. Observing the helpless stranger, he too hurried on his way. Eventually, a despised Samaritan approached the prostrate individual. Appraising the need, this *heretic* bound up the man's wounds, provided his own donkey, and took him to an inn where arrangements were made for his recovery.

"Which of these three do you think was a neighbor to the man who fell into the hands of robber?" Jesus inquired. The legal expert replied: "The one who had mercy on him." At which, Jesus responded: "Go and do likewise."

In this regard, we see ethics as response to human need, expedited by compassion. Millard Erickson consequently comments:

> Since love of neighbor is closely linked by the law to love of God and involves actions like those of the good Samaritan, the Christian church must be concerned about hurt and need in the world. Indeed, Jesus suggests in Matthew 25:31-46 that the one sign by which true believers can be distinguished from those who make empty professions is acts of love which are done in Jesus' name and emulate his example.[25]

This analysis invites us to look at *need* first, followed by *compassion*. Abraham Maslow provides us with a classic treatment of the former. In his *hierarchy of needs*, he identifies the following: life, safety and security, belonging and affection, respect and self-respect, and self-actualization.[26]

Life is fundamental to the rest. It is, as Maslow observes, the most urgent concern. Other needs can be postponed if necessary. Survival takes over. The priest and Levite got failing grades in this connection, while the Samaritan scored at the top of his class.

Safety and security mean to preserve *life*. Even so, Maslow points out that threatening (chaotic) conditions can actually strengthen individual resolve. As someone has said, it does not matter if we are in over our heads so long as we are not over God's head.

Belonging and affection extend our horizons. "If both the physiological and the safety needs are fairly well gratified, there will emerge the love and affection and belongingness needs, and the whole cycle already described will repeat itself with this new center."[27] On the other hand, one becomes increasingly aware of other things lacking--such as those needs yet to be addressed.

Among these are *the respect of others* and *respect of self*. All healthy people, according to Maslow, want to be esteemed by others and oneself. One is not adequate without the other. These, in turn, involve *competency* and *reputation*. As with the former duality, one does not suffice without the other.

Self-actualization rounds off the hierarchy of needs. "Even if all these needs are satisfied, we may still often expect that a new discontent and restlessness will soon develop, unless the individual is doing what *he*, individually, is fitted for."[28] This holds true in *fractal* (self-similar) fashion. In one connection, Maslow observes that an artist is never content unless given the opportunity to paint. In another, Augustine suggests that we feel empty unless filled by God.

None of the above needs must be thoroughly satisfied before we move on to consider others. As a matter of fact, we return to previous concerns better equipped for having addressed others. This is best thought of as a both/and endeavor.

As for *compassion*, "*Absolutely everything* is commanded which love requires, absolutely everything without the slightest exception or softening. *Freedom from* the law belongs only to that individual who is *free for* reason of the most terrifying obligation."[29]

The commandments to love God without qualification and one's neighbor as oneself belong together.

> The first entails the second; the second presupposes and depends on the first. ...In neither case is love construed as an emotion. Love for one's neighbor means acting toward others with their good, their well-being, their fulfillment, as the primary motivation and goal of our deeds.[30]

We must moreover bear in mind that there is always more than one neighbor. Otherwise, we will lavish our concern on some individual or select group, to the exclusion of others. The love of neighbor builds no fences, not even to keep out those who return evil for good.

In Retrospect

We observed at the outset that chaos theory provides a new and promising way of looking at things. With this in mind, we determined to review Christian ethics from chaos perspective. We hoped that in so doing we would come to better appreciate our moral obligation as Christians.

We subsequently introduced a passage from Jeremiah, where an impending disaster brings to mind primeval chaos. This alerts us to the fact that chaos continues to characterize life as we experience it. It also suggests that we expand our understanding of chaos as it impinges on ethical resolve.

After this, we explored five motifs concerning oughtness, reflection, creativity, discipleship, and one's neighbor. *Oughtness* reminds us that we perceive life not only as what exists, but how it should be improved upon. *Reflection* urges us to do so from the perspective of being created in God's image. *Creativity* details one aspect of being in God's image, namely with the capacity to innovate. *Discipleship* enrolls us in the school of the prophets, followed by graduate instruction in the school of Christ.

Concern for neighbor sets a meeting-of-needs agenda, fueled by compassion.

Chaos theory throws the above into sharper relief in various ways. First, we do not dismiss chaos out-of-hand. It can serve a positive purpose by strengthening our moral resolve. It additionally provides access to creative adaptation.

Second, chaos is not something we ought to extend needlessly. Whatever its merits, it can readily prove disabling. In this connection, we noted earlier Jesus' complaint: "They tie up heavy loads and put them on men's shoulders, but they themselves are not willing to lift a finger to move them" (Matt. 23:4).

Third, order (the law) pertains except where superseded by radical love. The latter can never require less than the former, and must in fact demand more. As sometimes put, love God and you will do His will; love others and you do His will.

Fourth, we look beyond both order and chaos in Christian ethics to God. There can be no final answers from chaos perspective, "but only more questions, with science providing procedures for addressing certain important and interesting classes of such questions."[31]

Finally, we press on with confidence that Christ breaks the chaos trail ahead. He likewise beckons us to follow Him, and in doing so, to embody the Christian ethic. This, in turn, reminds us that Christian ethics are not strictly speaking a code to follow but a relationship to be lived out.

Editorial note. This final article draws upon *Exhortations of Jesus According to Matthew* (1997) for its general orientation, and *Chaos Paradigm: A Theological Exploration* (1998) for its particular chaos formulation. As such, it is my most recent effort in both regards.

ENDNOTES

1. S. Neil Rasband, *Chaotic Dynamics as Nonlinear Systems*, p. 1.
2. Daniel Kaplan and Leon Glass, *Understanding Nonlinear Dynamics*, p. 27.
3. Derek Kidner, *Genesis*, p. 44.
4. John Casti, *Paradigms Lost*, p. 494.
5. Paul Davies, "Is the Universe a Machine?" *Exploring Chaos* (Hall, ed.), p. 221.
6. Philip Wheelwright, *A Critical Introduction to Ethics*, p. 1.
7. C.G. Montefiore, "Jesus and the Rabbis," *Jesus* (Anderson, ed.), p. 156.
8. Donald Ford and Richard Lerner, *Developmental Systems Theory*, p. 52.
9. Ibid., p. 85.
10. Donald Bloesch, *Freedom For Obedience*, p. 8.
11. Walter Brueggemann, *Genesis*, p. 46.
12. Kidner, *op. cit.*, p. 68.
13. Robert Seltzer, *Jewish People, Jewish Thought*, p. 197.
14. Arthur Patzia, *Ephesians, Colossians, Philemon*, p. 76.
15. Herbert Wolf, *An Introduction to the Old Testament Pentateuch*, p. 23.
16. Jacques Maquet, *The Aesthetic Experience*, p. 131.
17. Ibid.
18. Arnold Hauser, *The Social Theory of Art*, Vol. 1, p. 115.
19. Morris Inch, *Exhortations of Jesus According to Matthew* and *Up From the Depths*, p. 9.
20. Gardiner Day, *The Apostles' Creed*, p. 84.
21. Casti, *op. cit.*, p. 65.
22. Inch, *op. cit.*, p. 33.
23. Stephen Kellert, *In the Wake of Chaos*, p. 5.
24. Inch, *op. cit.*, p. 52.
25. Millard Erickson, *Christian Theology*, Vol. 3, p. 1058.
26. Abraham Maslow, *The Further Reaches of Human Nature*, p. 3.
27. Ibid., p. 43.
28. Ibid., p. 46.
29. Paul Ramsey, *Basic Christian Ethics*, p. 89.
30. Donald Hagner, *Matthew 14-28*, p. 648.
31. Casti, *op. cit.*, p. 66.

BIBLIOGRAPHY

Anderson, Hugh (ed.). *Jesus: Great Lives Observed.* Englewood Cliffs: Prentice-Hall, 1967.

Bloesch, Donald. *Freedom For Obedience.* San Francisco: Harper & Row, 1987.

Brueggemann, Walter. *Genesis.* Richmond: John Knox, 1982.

Casti, John. *Paradigms Lost.* New York: Morrow, 1989.

Davies, Paul. "Is the Universe a Machine?" *Exploring Chaos* (Hall, ed.), 211-221.

Day, Gardiner. *The Apostles' Creed: An Interpretation For Today.* New York: Scribners, 1963.

Erickson, Millard. *Christian Theology.* 3 vols. Grand Rapids: Baker, 1985.

Ford, Donald and Richard Lerner. *Developmental Systems Theory.* Newburg Park: Sage, 1992.

Hagner, Donald. *Matthew 14-28.* Dallas: Word, 1995.

Hall, Nina (ed.). *Exploring Chaos.* New York: Norton, 1991.

Hanson, Arnold. *The Social Heritage of Art.* 5 vols. New York: Heritage, 1985.

Inch, Morris. *Exhortations of Jesus According to Matthew* and *Up From the Depths: Mark as Tragedy.* Lanham: University Press of America, 1997.

Kaplan, Daniel and Leon Glass. *Understanding Nonlinear Dynamics.* Berlin: Springer-Verlag, 1995.

Kellert, Stephen. *In the Wake of Chaos.* Chicago: University of Chicago, 1993.

Kidner, Derek. *Genesis.* Downers Grove: Inter-Varsity, 1967.

Maquet, Jacques. *The Aesthetic Experience.* New Haven: Yale University, 1986.

Maslow, Abraham. *The Further Reaches of Human Nature.* New York: Harper & Row, 1970.

Montefiore, C.G. "Jesus and the Rabbis," *Jesus* (Anderson, ed.), 155-157.

Patzia, Arthur. *Ephesians, Colossians, Philemon.* Peabody: Hendrickson, 1993.

Ramsey, Paul. *Basic Christian Ethics.* New York: Scribners, 1954.

Rasband, S. Neil. *Chaotic Dynamics of Nonlinear Systems.* New York: Wiley, 1990.

Seltzer, Robert. *Jewish People, Jewish Thought.* New York: Macmillan, 1980.
Wheelwright, Philip. *A Critical Introduction to Ethics.* New York: Odyssey, 1959.
Wolf, Herbert. *An Introduction to the Old Testament Pentateuch.* Chicago: Moody, 1991.

APPENDIX: THE PAPER TRAIL

The paper trail will reveal that the parameters of my thinking concerning theological anthropology were set early on. In particular, with man created in God's image, flawed, realized in Christ, and restored through Him. Even so, there have been significant developments and at least one substantial restructuring--with chaos theory. The latter does not seem a departure from earlier convictions, but a more plausible way of understanding and expressing them.

Psychology in the Psalms:

"To know God as He is is to begin to understand one's self. Otherwise, man walks the peculiar twilight zone between beast and God. He is repulsed by the jungle code but sits uneasily on the throne of self-worship" (p. 13).

"The most pressing and persistent question for man concerns the nature of his existence. The question cries aloud for attention and pleads for resolution" (p. 13).

> Contemporary studies of man measure his affinity to brute beast, and trace his origin from the organic elements. ...Man, however, was formed not only from the dust of the ground but the breath of God. He needs to look up to gain perspective and discover that he is in the image of the Most High (p. 16).

"Jesus is the true man who is obedient to God and restores man to fellowship with Him (Heb. 2:9-11). Unfortunately man is reluctant to admit his defection or accept God's grace" (p. 17).

"Man's difficulty is not simply ignorance of his nature, but wilful disobedience of God. ...He needs not only reorientation but repentance. The only road is the road back" (p. 17).

"Man is responsible to God and liable for God's creation. Gratification is found in purpose, fulfillment in the responsible life" (p. 20).

"The psalmist was a rational man. He considers the meaning of the heavens, surveys the adversaries and the youthful ranks of the defenders, reflects on the feebleness and nobility of man, and magnifies the name of God" (p. 21).

> ·   The emotions of the psalmist are vividly expressed. There are the threshold feelings of the night--the coolness against his flesh, the soft whisper of air after a drying day, the earth oozing between his toes, the sound of a distant dog protesting an intrusion, the sparkle of light against the pitch-black sky.
>
> There were the intuitive feelings of the soul--the sense of unworthiness, the awareness of danger, the presence of God, the joy of being. There were the feelings accompanying understanding--the glory of the God who has revealed Himself, the safety of the people for whom God does battle, the perfection of God's purpose and plan for man (p.22).

"Man is a volitional creature. He is not simply acted upon, the product of external forces, but he acts, creating history and culture" (p. 22).

"They were men who thought, felt, and willed. Above all, they were men of faith. They realized the spiritual dimension of life, that they were made in God's image and for His purpose" (p. 22).

"The effects of human solidarity can hardly be exaggerated. The individual is one *of* and *with* mankind. The results of personal choice reenter as control, not only in the individual life, but as a social heritage" (p. 36).

"In flight from God man only succeeds in losing himself and experiences a state of profound uncertainty which gives rise to anxiety" (p. 39).

"He (man) is *homo alienatus*--alienated man. There is still in him the capacity for knowing God, but communion is lacking. He senses responsibility, but no longer perceives its nature or realizes its function" (p. 43).

"There is no merit to guilt *per se*, but only in its insistence that human ills be treated. ...When guilt has led man to God, it has fulfilled its divine mission" (pp. 47-48).

"The tragedy of human experience is countered with the triumph of Christ. Restoration is no further away than proclamation and the whispered response of faith" (p. 56).

"God's way is good. Accepting His prescription for life results in increased confidence in the way He sustains, in openness to the varied experiences of this way, in a developing fullness of living, and in a productive service" (p. 71).

"It is by living totally in the world that Christian personality is formed" (p. 73).

"Every foe of man is an enemy of God, and opposition to God is in the last analysis a threat to man" (p. 135).

"The persisting clue to history is the interpretation of event in the light of God's revelation, the record of divine challenge and human response. When man has seen the potential of the present, the past has achieved its pedagogical purpose" (p. 166).

"Hope is not blind because it lacks sight. Rather, it sees through the eyes of God and rejoices in His beneficent intent" (p. 179).

> Ethics, then, is situational, if we mean by this that decisions must at least in part reflect the unique character of the given situation. There are no pat answers, no godly gimmicks, no simple directions. Life is complex, and faith faces out on life (p. 181).

Christianity Without Walls:

"The life of responsibility Jesus advocates is in opposition to both license and legalism; it consists of both change and continuance; it considers people and not simply causes; it sees God as unqualified good, forgiving, and redemptive" (p. 21).

> What, if anything, is the difference between being a Christian and being an American? When faith can no longer call forth its object and the conditions of its trust, it is little more than faith in faith. It is living off a legacy which is slipping away and with it, a grasp on life itself (p.36).

"God gave man life, and we are to give our life back to Him. But giving life to God does not mean sacrificing our humanity; it is giving life *to* rather than giving life *up*" (p. 59).

"With the hindsight of God's work and the foresight of God's will, the church stands in a remarkably unique position to bring the eternal truth to bear on contemporary times" (p. 63).

"Good faith follows Jesus into the world of contradiction, apathy, and absurdity. While forsaking evil, good faith claims the world for Christ" (p. 64).

> Jesus was particularly concerned for society's outcasts, suffering, and handicapped. He bequeathed His ministry on their behalf to the church,

which in accepting the obligation, testifies...that life incorporates all people, not simply those who can most successfully compete for survival (p. 91).

Paced By God:

"Man is more human for being Christian, and increasingly responsible as his faith matures. Labor is performed as a service of worship, provision is made for the needs of his fellows, and life is extended without distinction" (p. 28).

"I am the sum total of my relationships. This fact does not detract from my origin, the uniqueness of my psyche, or the prospect of change. I simply am what I am" (p. 52).

> His (God's) words were uttered before the people could reflect on their meaning, and when they *heard* he had already passed on to related subjects. One gets a breathless feeling when he really takes God seriously, an impression of being somehow just a whisker behind him at any given point (p. 87).

> Jesus not only lived but with a zest which disturbed his meticulous contemporaries. He laughed with abandon over the antics of children, lingered over food spread before him, and luxuriated in the company of friends. Each step was a benediction on some aspect of life (p. 91).

"The nature of promise has become for him (Paul) a way of life. He greets each morning with the thought that this is the day of the Lord's appointing, and invests its moments with the potential which this implies" (p. 95).

> Anxiety is an extravagance which the runner cannot afford. If he frets about how he is doing, he races poorly; if he is distracted by the progress of others, he flounders. He must give his full attention to the performance itself, stretching his capabilities to the full (p. 98).

"Only when we no longer need the other in an ultimate sense can we relate in a mutually beneficial way. Then, we can...be in and for others, for we experience the reality of the Divine mystery made evident and accessible in Christ" (p. 120).

Celebrating Jesus as Lord:

"Others may not comprehend, may think us peculiar, but we know there is no better place than to be there at Jesus' feet, learning about Him, learning about life" (p. 23).

> The Christian life resembles marriage in that no simple set of rules can cover all the things that turn up. Rather you pledge that, in whatever eventuates, your love and devotion will remain constant, thus providing the needed inspiration to work through any difficulty (p. 46).

"Give and give cheerfully. Thank God, not just for what you received today, but for what you have been able to share with others. ...Celebrate life as an opportunity to give to God and to one another" (p. 60).

"We get the feeling that things are out of control, our grip on things has been lost, but the Master returns order to the chaos that has developed. The vision from the mountain top transforms service at its foot" (p. 70).

> Who is greatest in the kingdom of heaven? Look for yourself: a little child. ...Where had the child been when the followers weighed the implications of Jesus' teaching against their prior understanding of prominence? Perhaps he was watching a frog leap majestically from place to place, feeling the grass tickle his feet, sharing a story with a friend, living, and enjoying what God provides us to live with. He was so involved in life that there was little thought, and no concern, over whether he would gain a place nearer to heaven's throne, so near to God at the moment that eternity seemed no problem to him (p.76).

"What a delightful prospect: Jesus is Lord, and the whole, varied and challenging world is our parish!" (p. 125).

Understanding Bible Prophecy:

"God would speak today as his servants listen breathlessly, having pressed beyond prophecy as simple prediction to understanding it as the disclosure of God to man" (p. 9).

"The kingdom of God provided the necessary purchase for the prophets. It was their leverage on the most obstinate situation with which they thought to herald the rise and fall of nations and welcome a permanent order" (p. 56).

"The prophetic morality was religious in nature and expressed itself in relationship to justice, compassion for others, and concern for the issues with which they struggled" (p. 113).

> Who is the model of true spirituality? Not an excessively serene and equally rotund man who comes to mind. He has withdrawn from life as

to maintain a placid disposition and feels neither the hurt about him nor the concern of the Holy Spirit to heal the wounds inflicted on his fellow man. He is isolated but not separated.

Another model does better. He works with men who disdain his faith, ridicule him at times, practice indifference as a rule. He extends himself in service to any and all. He is a man of prayer and study, but not a recluse. His spirituality has a religious-social character. His is, I would gather, *true* spirituality (pp. 122-123).

The prophets "were sensitive to changing times and their obligations concerning them. They sensed that God never demands more or less of persons then is warranted, and they expected him to tip the scales in favor of those who trust him" (p. 136).

The Evangelical Challenge:

The point is that the early Christians were aware of their distinctive identity only as those who lived in the afterglow of the resurrection. The personal vindication of Jesus as Lord drew them into a fellowship of those of like precious faith, and cooperative ministry (p. 102).

"The world does not need broad generalities or pat answers. To be a true catalyst, the evangelical must learn to apply sensitively the abiding truths of Scripture to genuine needs at hand" (p. 110).

"The Christian faith appears to the evangelical as a stream flowing from its source in Christ. There may be a twist in its course now and then, some historical eddy, a curious diversion, but it remains essentially unaltered in its course" (p. 130).

Christians may find themselves on different sides of a given issue and pressing some partisan perspective. The evangelical sees nothing inconsistent with this lack of uniformity. ...Nevertheless, he would like to demonstrate a concern for social issues within a somewhat predictable range of responses (p. 131).

"What is the nature of our cultural enterprise? To pursue learning, virtue, and piety and so transcend the mere demand of organic necessity" (p. 149).

"A vital and vigorous church is the first evidence that we are fulfilling the cultural mandate. More specifically, the church must be able to recall the mandate, celebrate its importance, and act responsibly in connection with it" (p. 149).

My Servant Job:

> It comes as a surprise to many that the good they experience in life emanates from God, or that they can most fully appreciate it by cultivating a relationship with Him. ...God does not resemble the resident policeman so much as generous benefactor (p. 16).

"The simple good of the Creator plus the simple evil of the creature plus the redemptive purpose of God equal the complex good, to which accepted suffering and repented sin contribute" (p. 20).

"Freedom was never given to man in the sense he could exercise it on his own. But for God sustaining man in his freedom, he inevitably slips into slavery" (p. 27).

> We do well to allow God the prerogative of transcendence and to accept the ambiguity that results. One God is enough; we do not need to know everything about everything. God has revealed what is essential for our well-being, and we can trust Him for the rest (p. 48).

> To live beyond prejudice and sophistry, we need, by the grace of God, to welcome life in all its complexity, endless variety, and limitless possibilities. Job does well to press ahead for fear that he might miss some good thing that the Almighty holds in store for him (p. 72).

> The marks of the Master's hands are everywhere visible in the godly man: in his stalwart commitment to justice, his gentle compassion toward those in need, his perseverance with thankless tasks. Such signs of character take time and skill to bring about (p. 84).

"Job's curiosity about life's ultimate questions would have to wait, while his stewardship of life's opportunities took precedence" (p. 121).

Doing Theology Across Cultures:

"Only a high view of culture, which acknowledges the Bible as the Word of God, will allow God to rule" (p. 18).

> Given a high view of culture, the introduction of Christianity will have a direct effect on only a small minority of the cultural components-- whether to encourage, change, or prohibit them. A high view culture will also see in an individual culture an imperfect response to God's invitation to subdue the earth... (p. 22).

> When Scripture makes a pronouncement about generic man, there is a

transcultural principle involved. However, this transcultural principle is necessarily expressed in some cultural context, so that we must distinguish between the principle and the manner in which it is expressed (p. 41).

Salvation in the context of salvation history is not, nor could it ever be, a strictly private matter. We become part of what some have described as God's people moving through history. ...We assume a common historical legacy and a shared responsibility to pass it on to others (p. 64).

"Christian influence surges and retires. At the point of high tide it seems to sweep everything before it, but at low tide it appears too feeble to do more than lap at the cultural and political shoreline" (p. 98).

"Everyone is required to serve in the areas of his calling: if he is a son, he must be a good son; as a citizen, he must be a good citizen. In each of these areas he must model the Christian faith for others to see and witness to his faith that they might hear" (p. 99).

Saga of the Spirit:

"The problem with man is that he attempts to grasp life for himself instead of accepting it from God's gracious hand. He discovers the more he grasps, the less he has as a result" (p. 29).

"Freedom in the Spirit is a freedom to develop one's unique qualities, and so to enrich the rest of creation" (p. 32).

It seems best to cast the Spirit with reference to the cycle of deliverance as a whole, rather than as related to deliverance alone. He works redemptively with the...grim realities of a prodigal people of God, sometimes to chastise, on other occasions to console, and to deliver when the time is ripe (p. 38).

They (the covenant people) were to show no partiality, to resist special interests, and to oppose such power structures as would help some to profit at the expense of others... . It (justice) requires creative approaches to meeting the needs of the impoverished, the infirm, and the dispossessed (p. 39).

The Spirit appears in the midst of culture as the divine celebrant. Life is good--as it was declared in the creation narrative--in spite of the suffering that dogs its footsteps. No one knew this better than the people of God, encouraged to praise by the Spirit of God (p. 46).

What the people of Israel knew at this point was *where* to turn; what they did not know was precisely *how* God would achieve His purpose through a repentant people. ...(They) lacked the hindsight we enjoy. They could only turn from their perilous ways, seek His face, and trust in His benevolent purposes (p. 59).

However we explain the presence of morality, man seems incurably concerned with what he and others ought and ought not to do. There are also significant similarities. So, for example, while people may differ on their view of modesty, each has some opinion as to what is modest and what is not (p. 121).

The restless character of holiness can best be seen against the backdrop of its struggle with sin. It resists evil inclinations and offers encouragement to the more noble aspirations, refusing compromise with the world and fostering the communion of saints (p. 174).

It is the nature of the gospel that it triumphs over the powers, however they may be expressed in one culture or another. One must be prepared to leave all in order to follow Christ, whether the "all" involves a sacred tree in a primitive village or the organizational image of some industrial firm (p. 185).

Making the Good News Relevant:

"It (conversion) is a response that assumes the cultural and psychological orientation of the person involved. ...For instance, the conversion may be more intellectual, emotional, or volitional in character --while essentially holistic and personal" (p. 58).

"Discipleship is a lifelong experience with the call of Christ. We are ever learning, growing, and becoming. We can comfort ourselves with the thought that God is not through working with or through us" (p. 64).

Even in what appear to be our most solitary moments, we are not alone. Christ is with us, as are the thoughts and prayers of others. Thus we labor where others have worked before us, and in preparation for those who have yet to enter upon their work (p. 64).

We must resist in the process those who hope to plunge uncritically into the work (as if we were not charged to love our God with all our minds), or others who prefer ivory-tower discussion to concerted action. These are false alternatives meant to dissuade us from necessary aspects of our mission (p. 66).

Those caught in the pressures of urban living often reflect back on their earlier life in the village as if it were paradise lost. Of course, they have an unrealistic memory of the past, and the things were not as agreeable as

they recall. But feelings are more critical than facts at this juncture...
(p. 92).

"It seems evident that the earliest Christians understood their ministry
in holistic terms. No less than the prophets before them, they were
advocates of the Kingdom of God. ...But their emphasis was no less
Christocentric for its breadth of concern" (p. 99).

> Some are urging us to accommodate the gospel so as to make it
> culturally relevant. We think this at best a one-sided concern; at worst a
> compromise of the faith. ...We freely admit that one can err on the other
> side, by failing to appreciate the integrity of the receptor culture (p. 100).

Revelation Across Cultures:

"God created man, not the Hebrew as such. Repentant Adam was not
a Hebrew, nor noble Enoch, nor righteous Noah, and not strictly speaking
even father Abraham. God was and is sovereign of all; God was and is
concerned for all" (p. 27).

"With God, even the seemingly impossible is within reach; without
God, we attempt one step forward and slip back two" (pp. 74-75).

"Self-renunciation was only one side of discipleship; affirmation of the
Kingdom provides the other" (p. 76).

"Jubilee typology called forth the most noble aspirations within Jewish
tradition, not least of which was concern for the poor. This was
reinforced by the example and teaching of Jesus, who assisted others
with little concern for Himself" (p. 79).

"An upright disposition ought to be reflected in the practice of justice.
The lack of justice suggests a spiritual problem of serious proportion"
(p. 79).

"What was lost through sin, God offers to redeem. What He redeems,
He makes righteous. Imputed righteousness is by Biblical definition
righteousness that surpasses ritual observance" (p. 82).

"Christian faith is more than intellectual assent. It implies a rigorous
commitment, discipline, and service" (p. 90).

> The American experiment illustrates the comprehensive fashion in
> which revelation impacts on culture. It does so first and foremost in a
> confessional setting. This involves a community which serves to
> cultivate a religious legacy.
>
> Revelation also infuses civic life by introducing acceptable social
> mores, legal precedents, correction modes, and divine sanctions--whether
> explicit or implicit. It provides a foundation which if disregarded

threatens societal order and security.

Revelation finally pervades popular culture. It becomes part of what we read, listen to on radio, look at on television, and share together in our conversation. It also tends to cultural accommodation at the expense of traditional faith (p. 109).

Charting a Good Church Trip:

He (Jesus) was said to have fully lived out in His own life what He taught others. ....The disciples suffered by comparison. They "were unschooled, ordinary men" (Acts 4:13). This is not to say that they were illiterate, but untrained in the finer aspects of the Torah. ...They were sometimes prejudiced. This came out in their dealings with the Samaritans (Luke 9:54; cf. Luke 10:25-37). ...The disciples were often perplexed. Peter struggled with how many times one should forgive his brother who sins against him (Matt. 18:21). ...They were not dependable. ...They were without exception sinful (pp. 6-7).

"God was the source of power; the disciples (individually and corporately) its recipients; the world its beneficiary" (p. 15).

Fact: Jesus never promised that we would experience the fellowship of other Christians. When we do so, we ought to consider it in the nature of a bonus. ...*Fact*: Qualifications aside, there is nothing unspiritual about desiring fellowship with others. It is natural, healthy, and profitable" (pp. 24-25).

"The mix of metaphors is also striking: the Church being expressed both as God's people and His temple, both community and institution. In a manner of speaking, it reveals two faces" (p. 40).

Spirituality, it bears repeating, amounts to living out God's will in our lives, through the intercession of Christ, by the enabling power of the Spirit. It is not something we accomplish by ourselves, nor is it thrust upon us--as if our cooperation were unnecessary (p. 50).

"Draw near to God. In so doing, we will be drawn to each other. Failing to do so, we remain far apart even when meeting together. Gathering in itself does not constitute community or communion" (p. 54).

God is more inclined to reward the earnest sermonic effort than the technically refined alternative, pompously delivered. He also delights in satisfying those who long to hear and obey His word. The faithful sermon and searching congregation form a combination hard to rival (p. 68).

> The Spartan warrior who fell in battle was carried home on his shield, to the acclaim of the populace; the Christian martyr was displayed in contempt. The Spartan warrior was eulogized and given a honorable burial; the Christian martyr discarded as refuse. The Spartan warrior's family was praised for making a noble sacrifice; the Christian martyr's family was left in disgrace. So suffered the Christian faithful (p. 81).

> This is *His* world, every shrub and pebble on the beach. We confuse matters by talking about our life, our possessions, or our rights. The only life we have God has given and sustains; our only possessions we hold as stewards; the only rights we enjoy must be used responsibly. Either we learn to live in God's world or we live an illusion (p. 98).

Exhortations of Jesus According to Matthew:

"'Come follow me.' Only three words, they speak a volume. They characterize Jesus' Messianic appeal; all else resembles commentary" (p. 11).

> As for Jesus' disciples, they do not as a rule seem to share Matthew's dubious background. Peter and Andrew, as cases in point, appear as God-fearing people engaged in constructive enterprise. We must conclude that Jesus called persons indiscriminate of virtue to follow Him (p. 13).

"When drawing similarities between Jesus' teaching and that of others we muddy the water. As the Anointed of God, He was unique; as were His exhortations so understood. They require that we lay aside not only the evil but good to serve the ultimate" (p. 16).

"Righteousness resembles an investment in eternity. It also contributes to a full and rewarding life. The righteous stand to gain whether in life or through death. God is no person's debtor" (p. 22).

"Jesus does not admonish the community to give alms, pray, and fast, but how they should do so. These three acts of religious devotion have been fundamental to Jewish piety over the years. Conversely, they are not always properly motivated" (p. 36).

"Do not babble on as the pagans are prone to do. They think that prayer has efficacy in and of itself. They suppose that there is merit to lengthy prayer. Neither is true. Prayer serves only as it expresses communion with God" (p. 37).

"Our social responsibilities are bound inexorably to our religious devotion. They grow out of our recognition that all were created in God's image and for His pleasure. There can be no exception, either within or without the household of faith" (p. 39).

"Jesus urged those who had *come* in faith to *go* in service. The world owed them nothing; they were committed to Christ for the world in everything" (p. 43).

"While there is much in the world to distract us, press on. While there are those who would dissuade us, press on. While discouraged by events, keep pressing on. There is a light at the end of the tunnel" (p. 51).

> It seems obvious that Jesus intended the disciples to live in creative tension with the world. They were caught as if between heaven and earth. Their heads being in the clouds, their feet must remain firmly on the ground. In this regard, they were true heirs of the lamenting prophets (pp. 60-61).

Up From the Depths:

"The prophets were uncompromising advocates of the covenant, painfully aware of the disparity that existed, insistent that the people must repent, and confident of God's willingness to forgive. Jesus would be no less so" (p. 74).

"Out of the depths, we cry for deliverance. Up from the depths, He would deliver us. Expectantly into the future, He would guide us. Thus the tragic hero snatches spiritual victory out of seeming defeat" (p. 80).

"Where some tragic heroes clearly are flawed, Jesus was not one of these. Where some imperceptibly are flawed, Jesus was not among them. Where some suffered because of circumstances voluntarily assumed, Jesus served as a prime case in point" (p. 82).

"The kingdom *has* come as an earnest; the kingdom *will* come in its fullness. One can live toward the future, but not indefinitely cling to the past" (p. 94).

"We have met the enemy, and he is us. We cannot blame our dilemma on others" (p. 103).

"The rabbis reasoned that three combine in creating life: God, father, and mother. Those who honor father and mother, honor God" (p. 107).

"As mentioned earlier, the *crisis* serves to separate the disciples from the rest. They become the insiders; others remain outside. They assume heroic character if only to a modest extent" (p. 125).

> Death conceivably was not the worst scenario. Given the disciples' cultural disposition, losing face could be worse. Being cut off from one's people was virtually intolerable. Bringing disgrace on one's family held

a horrifying prospect. Each time fear tugged at their heart strings, they responded with another step toward Jerusalem. So it is with faith, one step at a time. Having decided to follow Jesus, they were determined not to turn back (p. 139).

When pity has drawn us to the foot of the cross, faith can take over" (p. 148).

"Our personal agendas are of little consequence. They appear as if footprints lost in the sands of time" (p. 165).

Sage Sayings:

"*Live and let live.* Live out your life as you see fit, and permit others the same privilege. Martin Luther reasoned that each person's vocation is so demanding that if we take our duties seriously we will have no time to second-guess others" (p. 12).

"*This is the first day of the rest of your life.* We are less the victims of fate than faulty choices. We can start a promising new course from this day forward" (p. 15).

"*We do not know what tomorrow brings.* No matter! It is not important to know what the future holds, so long as we know Who holds our future" (p. 19).

"*Change with the times.* The Hausa say: 'When the music changes so does the dance.' To live is to welcome change within the providence of God" (p. 21).

"*Hospitality is an expression of Divine worship* (Talmudic). When we welcome others, we welcome God as well. When we close the door to others, we also close our door to God" (p. 26).

Man does not live by bread alone. The second half of the Biblical reference is missing in the secular version: "...but on every word that comes from the mouth of God" (Matt. 4:4). ...To paraphrase Augustine: "God created in us a need that only His presence can satisfy" (p. 27).

"*Only when you have endured suffering do you remember God* (Hausa). C.S. Lewis observed that while God whispers to us in our joys, He shouts at us in our pain. Suffering gets our attention when all else fails" (p. 38).

"*Godliness with contentment is great gain* (1 Tim. 6:6). Contentment does not stand alone as a virtue. We are to strive to be godly and contented with what God provides as a means" (p. 42).

"*It is not how long but how well you live.* Measure life qualitatively rather than quantitatively. Some people pack a lot of living into a little time" (p. 59).

"*Years know better than books* (Romanian). Experience is the best teacher. We are encouraged to participate in life rather than sit back as an observer" (p. 70).

"*Two heads are better than one.* I often told students: 'If we thoroughly agree, one of us is not necessary.' Look at a subject first from one perspective and then another. Our understanding will be enriched in the process" (p. 79).

"*Whoever trades in lies will pay in truth* (Hausa). We cannot deceive the Almighty. He deals in truth alone" (p. 99).

> *It is more blessed to give than receive* (Acts 20:35). The joys and rewards associated with giving far outweigh those from receiving. Our society needs to look beyond its crusade for rights to focus on responsibilities which offer the opportunity for individual and corporate fulfillment (p. 105).

A Case For Christianity:

"If God gave us a mind, no doubt he intended us to use it. We ought not to claim more for our investigative powers than our finite condition warrants, but even so, these provide us with some means to evaluate rival claims to revealed truth" (p. 9).

"Some of us are much less optimistic concerning the perfectibility of humankind left to its own devices. Our successes seem more in the realm of technology than basic morality" (p. 47).

"Do not seek suffering; seek rather to serve God. Should the latter entail suffering, accept it graciously. Know that pain can purge the spirit and further our Christian witness" (p. 63).

"What is unique about humans? Four characteristics have been widely acknowledged: (1) complex symboling, (2) refined tool usage, (3) moral inclination, and (4) religious orientation" (pp. 65-66).

> We may conclude that hope is related to childish fantasy...to be put way as we mature. Or we may decide that circumstances have robbed us of fulfillment: the failure of parents, lack of appreciation from our employer, or choice of an insensitive spouse. There is finally the Christian option: if there is nothing in this life which corresponds to hope, as food to hunger or sex to the sexual drive, then hope is most likely associated with an unfulfilled potential in the future life (p. 76).

"Where Scripture speaks, we should affirm. Where Scripture does not speak, we should be cautious. We ought neither to lag behind nor rush ahead of biblical revelation" (p. 101).

"The good news for world religions in the context of progressive revelation is that they may embody truth in the process of being refined. The bad news is that they may represent premature closure" (p. 120).

> The "leap" of faith is perhaps an unfortunate metaphor. It would seem to imply a blind plunge into the unknown. Faith resembles more of a calculated trust.   When enough substantial evidence has been accumulated, an appropriate decision seems called for (p. 129).

"We do not have the choice between faith and unbelief. We can only choose between rival faiths. Such arguments as may be leveled against faith, as such, cut all ways. We are all entered on the same course: to discover a credible faith" (p. 132).

In Tune With God:

"We seem unable to tolerate the secular spirit for long. When orthodox faith wanes, people often turn to spiritualism and astrology to serve their religious disposition" (p. 36).

"He (man) was a marvel of creation, meant to commune with God and act as steward over all around him. The enormity of man's fall can only be appreciated in the light of his high estate and magnificent calling" (p. 39).

"Christians march to a different drum beat. They are not to conform to the world, but be transformed by the regenerating power of the Holy Spirit. This is the bottom line. All else is commentary" (p. 75).

"*Higher ground* has military connotations for me. ...We struggle up a ridge in anticipation of being able to carry the conflict to the enemy. ....Having gained our immediate goal, we can forge and implement a strategy" (p. 83).

"We have not genuinely learned how to live until prepared to die. Life and death interact in our experience" (p. 92).

"I encourage people not to worry about the *severity* of God's judgment. Worry instead about His justice. You may have conned others; you will not con Him" (pp. 94-95).

> ...Heaven is said to be a place of reward. ...(It is) likely spiritual in character, and would appeal only on that condition. C.S. Lewis captures this notion by describing persons from hell taking a picnic in heaven. They find it not at all to their liking, and cut their stay short.
> ...Heaven provides relief from the trials of this life. "He will wipe

every tear from their eyes. There will be no more death or mourning or crying or pain, for the old order of things has passed away" (Rev. 21:4).
...Heaven provides fulfillment. ...Former inhibitions will be a thing of the past. We shall be free to realize our true potential. There will be an explosion of virtue.
...Central to the rest, heaven will be living in God's presence. "Now the dwelling of God is with men, and he will live with them" (Rev. 21:3).
...Hell is a place of antithesis. It is everything heaven is not (pp. 95-96).

Chaos Paradigm:

"*Chaos* appears in Scripture at the outset, and as a reoccurring phenomenon. It pervades life. We cannot hope to escape chaos, but must learn to deal constructively and creatively with it" (p. 71).

"We ought not to invite chaos. It will come soon enough. When it does, we ought to use the opportunity to learn God's ways more perfectly" (p. 71).

"Even so, we ought not to unnecessarily extend the chaos experience. As suggested earlier, we press on through the wilderness to the promised land. Anything less would be to draw back from God's leading" (p. 71).

"There are usually harbingers to chaos. Life as we have experienced it begins to come apart. We build our defenses higher in hopes of buying time. In the end, it is to no avail" (p. 71).

"Once order begins to emerge, it needs to be cultivated. ...Nothing worthwhile comes easily, and especially when it involves charting a new course" (p. 72).

> Chaos, in Biblical perspective, involves a mix of *referents*. ...The *sea* is a prime referent. ...The *wilderness* is another. ...*Silence* is yet another. ...*Darkness* is a reoccurring referent. ...*Death* serves as a final vivid referent. ...The more one reads from chaos perspective, the more evident it becomes that chaos imagery is pervasive (p. 72).

> From a chaos perspective, we have known of chaos for thousands of years, but have hardly begun to consider it in the light of contemporary chaos theory. It seems that we should welcome a lively discussion, not for fear that someone is invading our privileged domain, but with the conviction that all truth is God's truth (p. 73).

"Given the sensitivity of nonlinear systems to original conditions, the results could be catastrophic. The dogma of original sin hence becomes eminently plausible from chaos perspective" (p. 81).

"Two contrasting ways stretch out before us: the way of life and death.

The way of life resembles a narrow path leading into ever broader opportunities; the latter a broad road narrowing to the point that we have no leeway" (p. 83).

> Sometimes there is little high ground from which to operate. At such time, we ought not to expect too much too soon. Capture some point of advantage even though it hardly seems worth the effort. This will open up more promising possibilities, more readily available (p. 83).

"Pascal's famous wager seems more convincing in chaos perspective than ever before. If God exists, we have all to gain in this life and that to come. If not, we have experienced the best this life has to offer. If however we fail to wager, we lose everything" (p. 86).

"After all has been said and done, we assert an anthropology for the real world" (p. 87).

> What a chimera (in Greek mythology, a fire belching monster with the head of a lion, the body of a goat, and a serpent's tail--likened by Pascal to man)! Created in the image of God reflecting something of his noble origin. Creative as well as created. Without focus unless focused in the Almighty.
>
> What a chimera! A rebel without a cause. Turning his back on God. Continuing in his perverse way without thought of the result on himself or others. Leaving behind a trail of destruction.
>
> What a chimera! Fallen but not forsaken. Still the object of God's love. Invited to respond to God's gracious initiatives. By God's grace, still redeemable." (p. 88).